Praise for *To Have and Not to Hold*

"Anyone touched by adoption needs to read this book and inhale Lorri's story. Lorri's circumstances as a 26-year-old employed woman are not completely typical of women who find themselves with an unplanned pregnancy. However, her emotional experiences of learning of her pregnancy, forming a relationship with her unborn baby, grappling with her options within herself and with people in her life, and finally making a decision after Aimee's birth DO completely represent the truth of each birthmother's journey. Board members and staff of adoption organizations should especially take note: adoption is not a transaction. Our obligation is to recognize and honor the fact that the decision to make an adoption plan becomes a part of the fabric of each birthparent's life. And it is a powerful fabric indeed."

—*Julie Tye, president of The Cradle (Adoption Agency and Services, Evanston, IL)*

"Adoptions are a different as fingerprints. No two are alike. *To Have and Not to Hold* is a lesson in listening to heart and conscience and staying true to oneself. Lorri Antosz Benson takes the reader on an emotional journey as she struggles with the decision to place baby Aimee up for adoption.

"While the pivotal act may be the giving up of Aimee for placement, the account of the following years and living with the consequences of the placement are filled with honest longing for the child she never knew. This is a wonderful story of possibilities when there is faith in the future and unselfish love for a child. As an adoptive mom, I marveled at the openness of adoptive mom Anne as she tentatively began to allow Lorri into her family's lives. *To Have and Not Hold* is a roadmap for what can happen when birthparents and adoptive parents put aside their fears. These moms took a chance and created a new family. This is a must-read for all parents."

—*Carol Ann Story, adoptive mother and former* CBS This Morning *book editor*

"I wept with joy reading Lorri Antosz Benson's eloquent and raw narrative *To Have and Not to Hold*. It provides <u>undeniable</u> proof that the universe makes no mistakes. Each and every one of us was always meant to be."

—Mary Beth McAdaragh, adoptee and National Media Marketing Executive

"Lorri Benson shares her deeply moving story of surrendering her baby in 1981 in a classically closed adoption, and of her moving persistently over time with the support of the adoptive mother to opening the adoption and first meeting her daughter when she was sixteen. *To Have and Not to Hold* is a testament to the power of trust and opening hearts. It also shows the evolving shifts in policy and practice over the years and how open adoption at its best is normalized like other blended families."

—Lynn C. Franklin, first/birth mother and author of May the Circle Be Unbroken: An Intimate Journey Into the Heart of Adoption

to have

AND NOT

to hold

Published by Familius LLC, www.familius.com

Familius books are available at special discounts for bulk purchases, whether for sales promotions or for family or corporate use. For more information, contact Familius Sales at 559-876-2170 or email orders@familius.com.

Library of Congress Cataloging-in-Publication Data
2016942948

Print ISBN 9781942934813
Ebook ISBN 9781944822217
Hardcover ISBN 9781944822224

Printed in the United States of America

Edited by Michele Robbins
Cover design by David Miles
Book design by Lindsay Sandberg and Maggie Wickes

10 9 8 7 6 5 4 3 2 1

First Edition

LORRI ANTOSZ BENSON

to have

AND NOT

to hold

The Bonding *of* Two Mothers
through Adoption

FAMILIUS

To June and Leo Antosz:

I don't even know yet the depths of how much you will be missed.

Your example of love and family serves as the backbone of who I am.

Ding Hao!

Contents

foreword

Very early in this beautifully rendered and often painfully sad story, Lorri decides to offer her newborn for adoption. While still in the hospital, immediately after giving birth, she writes:

> I tried to keep Aimee in my room
> as much as possible. I took photographs,
> knowing well these would be the only
> pictures of her I would have for a
> long time, if not forever. I would lay on
> my bed for hours, knees bent, with her on my legs,
> staring into her perfect face and
> talking to her about the life she would have.
> I would watch her sleep, marveling
> at her tiny nose and lovely eyelashes.
> And I would tell her I loved her.

The older I get, the easier I cry; now I'm already into the Kleenex. What follows on these pages is the flat-out naked true story of a twenty-something female who had it all: good job (ahem, she worked for me), handsome boyfriend, big city romantic evenings, loving parents, and ski-champion good looks.

Lorri was also a devout, never-miss-Sunday-Mass Catholic. She didn't consider acquiring protection from the consequence of a mortal sin she didn't intend to commit.

Kaboom! She's pregnant.

Ho, hum—you've heard this story before? No, no, no. You have not heard this story. The characters are all here: the kind woman at the adoption agency, the biological father who can't seem to commit to any option, and the parents who resolutely stand by Lorri and then retreat when first meeting their new granddaughter—defending against the pain of holding a child they know they will never hold again.

Also in the cast of this drama are Lorri's coworkers at the *Donahue* program office who unanimously wanted her to keep the baby. One male staffer with a soft, Italian heart whispered to me on an elevator, "Me and the Mrs.—we'll take the baby." Only after reading this book did I realize that our well-intentioned pleadings were for the outcome we wanted, revealing an unintended disrespect for what Lorri wanted for herself and for her baby.

To Have and Not to Hold boosts us all high enough to peek over the wall that surrounded the author during this deep and very personal drama. We become witnesses to the moral courage of a cast of people who know what love means, most especially the mother who was the answer to Lorri's prayers—the mother who adopted Lorri's baby and fiercely loves the daughter who is like her own flesh.

Also peeking over that wall will be Lorri's coworkers, including me. We will see how wrong we were in urging her not to surrender her baby. When we put this book down for the final time and discard the empty Kleenex box, Lorri will have shown us how unselfishly and courageously right she was.

And all the other readers will stare into space and know they have just been treated to a beautiful love story.

—Phil Donahue

life changer

November 8, 1981

"**O**www!"

I woke up with a start, sitting straight up on the thin mattress of my pullout sofa bed.

What in the world was that? In a fog, I looked over at the LED digits on the alarm clock. One o'clock a.m. I tried to remember what it was that woke me up and what day it was. As my head started to clear, another sharp pain took my breath away.

Okay, okay, this doesn't feel like a Braxton-Hicks, I told myself. The contractions I'd felt and worried about in the past month were child's play compared to the powerful grip that was squeezing the life out of my abdomen now. Was this it?

It was November 8, 1981: six days past my due date. Yes, this was it. I reached toward my nightstand for my trusty stopwatch. I'd taken it home from work every night for the past three weeks, just in case. That morning, I'd used it to time a TV segment with the Bee Gees. Now I was using it to see if my baby was on its way.

I drifted off waiting for the next contraction, watch in hand. Forty-five minutes later, I was jolted from sleep by the baby's not-at-all-gentle reminder that the waiting was about to be over. Checking the minute hand, I realized that I didn't really know for sure just when one actually went to the hospital. I had an hour's drive, though, and one thing was for sure—I didn't want to wait too long and have this baby on the highway.

My parents were sleeping in the next room, having arrived a few days earlier to help me during the birth. Each night, they'd given me instructions to wake them when "it was time." I was pretty sure they didn't mean after two contractions in the middle of the night. I picked up the phone, feeling a little reluctant to call anyone at two in the morning.

"I'm really sorry to call so late," I apologized to the voice at the other end of the line. "I may be in labor, and I thought I better call Dr. Morgan."

There was no hesitation from the experienced operator from my doctor's answering service. "How long between contractions?" she asked crisply.

"Umm," I stalled, suddenly feeling like I'd probably called a tiny bit too soon. "Forty-five minutes," I finally admitted, trying to sound like this was a perfectly acceptable response.

"Wait until five minutes apart," she instructed, "unless your water breaks; then come right in."

"But I live in Chicago," I protested, with undisguised panic in my voice. "I'm an hour from the hospital! Don't I have to come in sooner? How can I know for sure if this is really labor? What if I wait too long?"

She paused for a second or two. "Is this your first baby?" she asked. I knew she'd already guessed the answer.

"Yes," I muttered, to which she immediately replied with authority, "First babies always take a while. Five minutes apart will be plenty of time. And look for the bloody show."

Not willing to appear like a complete imbecile, I thanked her, hung up the phone, and wondered what the heck a bloody show was. Why hadn't I asked the doctor for more explicit instructions for game day?

With nothing else to do, I lay back down on my bed of strategically placed pillows with a notebook and the stopwatch and tried to relax. My bag had been packed for a week now, and I was as ready as I'd ever be. The night passed in a foggy cycle of sleeplessness. Just as I'd start to nod off, another death grip would jar me awake. I'd search frantically for the watch, which would have invariably fallen from my fingers. After flipping on the light for the tenth time, I finally got a flashlight so, without completely waking up, I could record the time elapsed since the last contraction.

By five thirty, I couldn't put it off any longer. The pains were coming around eight minutes apart, and a trip to the bathroom had introduced me to the world of bloody shows. I took a quick shower and beautified myself as only a hugely pregnant woman, who has had no sleep and is about to give birth, can do.

I crept into my own darkened bedroom and shook my parents awake, answering my mother's "Are you sure?" with a patiently tolerant tone: "Of course, Mom." No need to mention my confusion and total ignorance from hours before.

We were on the road by six o'clock, making a quick stop at my boyfriend Andrew's apartment to tell him we were on the way to the hospital. As my mother ran up and knocked on the door, I lay in the backseat of my dad's car. I was on a towel spread to protect the Cadillac's leather seats in the event of an unexpected surge of amniotic fluid. Or worse. I fought back the urge to scream as another searing wave of pain spread through me. I waved weakly to Andrew as he wished me well from his front door.

An hour later, we were walking into Sherman Hospital in Elgin, Illinois. The infamous Chicago potholes and I-290's well-traveled and rough roads had not done much for my mood, but I was happy to be there and pleased that my contractions were now the requested five minutes apart.

Things were happening faster now. Everything was going according to plan, and I hadn't had any time to second-guess myself. My focus was on having this baby and getting someone to make the pain go away. The labor room was tiny and nondescript. Being from a different generation, my father soon excused himself from the claustrophobic commotion in the room.

My savior walked into the room soon after all the check-in, assessment, and wardrobe changes had taken place. "Dr. Morgan!" I shouted in relief. "Thank goodness! How about that paracervical block we discussed?"

It was after ten o'clock in the morning, and I'd about had it with the constantly recurring, womb-ripping pain. It was 1981, after all—I saw no reason why a woman should need to feel every aspect of a child bursting through her body. It didn't help that I was now hooked up to a monitor and could literally watch with fear and dread as each contraction approached. Plus, I wanted to get the block before my Lamaze coach made her entrance and started in on her whole "natural breathing" regime. I didn't want anyone to get in the way of my drugs!

Dr. Morgan calmly smiled, introduced himself to my mother, and looked over my chart. "Well, let's see . . . your first contraction was at one in the morning . . . you've had a long night, haven't you?" I looked at him, stifling the impulse to say "Enough small talk . . . inject already!" and instead answered, "Yes, I'm pretty tired and ready to stop feeling like this."

My mother kissed me and left the room while Dr. Morgan conducted his examination. After explaining the process one more time, he administered the highly anticipated paracervical block and, finally, I felt some much-needed relief. Epidurals were not in use yet, and the blocks were Dr. Morgan's method of choice.

"You're textbook," he said proudly, as if I had something to do with this accomplishment. "You're moving right through dilation, and the baby is in perfect position."

"Well, thank you," I replied, happy that the onslaught of pain had begun to wane. "That's great news." As I asked him to bring my mom back into the tiny room, Mariellen, my Lamaze coach, strolled in with a smile on her face. Andrew and I had spent six Wednesday nights with her, learning breathing techniques and practicing for the main event. We were honest with her from the beginning—that this wasn't your average situation—and by the second session, knowing Andrew couldn't face being in the delivery room, I asked her to be my delivery coach.

"Wow, you look terrific!" she exclaimed. I knew I'd asked her to be here for a reason.

"Well, I just got a block," I confessed. "You should have seen me an hour ago." I cringed slightly, knowing her career was all about helping women have natural births. I still felt a tiny bit guilty, but I'd warned her ahead of time that she would most definitely have a pharmaceutical assistant.

"Hmmph," she snorted. "Oh, well; your breathing will still come in handy. Andrew called me so early; I thought I might be too late."

"Nope, plenty of time," Dr. Morgan interjected as he left to find my mother. I looked at Mariellen, frowning at the doctor's remark. She smothered a smirk and glanced at my chart.

"Don't worry," she reassured me, "you're already seven centimeters! This will all be over before you know it." Her grin faded and her eyes shifted quickly away from me, as though she'd said the wrong thing. I just smiled at her and looked over as the monitor leapt into action and a painless contraction began. In the past months, I'd gotten used to people feeling awkward around me.

The next few hours were a blur of breathing, being poked and prodded by the doctor and nurses, and talking on and off with my parents and Mariellen. Anything to keep my mind off the elephant in the room. And then it was time.

"Ten centimeters," Dr. Morgan crowed. "Time to push!" My mother joined my dad in the waiting room while my small entourage pushed my gurney into the delivery room. A different kind of pain began coursing through me, and Mariellen grabbed my hand, orchestrating my breathing as I began the final phase of childbirth.

It didn't take long from there. After only two or three pushes, Dr. Morgan quietly announced that he could see the head. As the next contraction came, I bore down with all my might, there was a searing pain, and then the head was there. With one more push and a swoosh, before I could comprehend what was actually happening, Dr. Morgan was holding my baby in his hands! Dark hair, tiny fingers, all ten of them outstretched, and everything where it should be. Perfection. A small cry. And the words "It's a girl!"

Mariellen gasped. "Oh, Lorri, she is just beautiful." She was—so beautiful. She took my breath away. I looked at her with tears brimming.

"Aimee Elizabeth," I murmured, giving her the name I'd chosen if the baby was a girl. "A beautiful gift from God." Dr. Morgan looked at me carefully. We had decided to play this part by ear.

"Do you want to hold her?" he asked tenderly. There was a sympathetic silence in the room.

"YES, I really, really do," I whispered, the tears now freely flowing. He carefully placed her on top of me, and I gathered her up, the umbilical cord still attached. She was still, momentarily, a part of me. She was a living, breathing part of me, and she was crying softly . . . and so tiny . . . and so angelic.

My baby was here. How had I ever imagined I wouldn't hold her? How could I have known she would cling to me like this and that I would love her with a force so powerful—like nothing I'd ever felt before?

Now I just had to figure out how I was going to give her away.

nine months is a lifetime

February 1981

C *ould life be any better than this?* I asked myself. When I graduated from Miami University in Ohio three and a half years earlier, I could have only dreamed about being where I was now.

After college, in 1977, I had immediately started work in Dayton, Ohio, where I had a comfortable room in my parents' home. I worked at a large retail store in the radio-TV ad department, but when they had to cut back just months later, I found myself on the buying floor. My complete lack of interest in retail buying dovetailed nicely with my back-burner itch to sow some ski-bum oats in Colorado before I settled into my career. It wasn't the plan my parents had in mind, but I set out for Colorado and ended up spending a valuable ski season in Vail, where I learned two things: how to ski the bumps and trees and that I needed more out of life than skiing the bumps and the trees.

After exploring options in several cities, I ended up in the Windy City working eighteen months at WGCI-TV, a small, crazy multi-platform UHF television station, where I put my newly acquired radio-TV-film degree to use as a director. In one day, I could stage-manage a financial show, direct a

Greek variety show complete with goats and chickens, and then use my pidgin Spanish-speaking skills to decipher when the decidedly NOT bilingual Mexican talk show host wanted to make his entrance. I paid my dues, and that investment definitely paid off. In May of 1980, I landed a job at *Donahue* as the associate producer on the *Today Show* segments that Phil Donahue hosted. I still had to pinch myself. PHIL DONAHUE . . . only the most brilliant man on the air and host of the hottest show on daytime television. I wasn't sure how I had hit this lottery; I only knew I was so grateful for this chance to prove myself in my chosen field.

I moved from my tiny Lincoln Park studio to a great one-bedroom apartment in a Gold Coast high-rise. I could walk to work at the exciting Merchandise Mart, which housed our NBC studio. While our *Donahue on Today* staff was small, I got to know the much larger group of *Donahue* employees who worked the main show from offices located at CBS. I had become part of a warm, close, highly dynamic work family headed by one of the most generous and talented people I have ever met.

It was amazing to go to work every day and not only work with Phil but also book and meet all the newsmakers of the day. It was exciting and challenging, and I didn't mind the long hours at all. I was, after all, at that point in my career where work was pretty much my life, and I was in an industry that demanded early starts, late nights, and being available if needed on the weekends. On top of that, I was working with the best of the best, and that required my dedication and commitment. I was happy to comply with all of this. After all, I was twenty-four, single, on my own in Chicago, and living it up enjoying my independence.

Fast forward to February 1981. Nine months after I started my job at *Donahue*, I had added Andrew, a nice, fun boyfriend, to the mix. He was literally tall, dark, and handsome, and for about the last four months or so, we had slowly progressed through dating to a more exclusive arrangement. We didn't talk that much about it; we just seemed to spend more and more time together.

Chicago was a thriving, exhilarating city with lots to do, and Andrew and I did all of it. We both were committed to our work, but on weekends, we kept the restaurants in business and took advantage of everything Chicago offered. We also took weekend trips, often up to his family's home in Wisconsin, where he had a boat on a beautiful lake. There was many a weekend spent waterskiing and having fun with his family. And now that we were solidly in the cold of winter, we took on winter sports and evenings by the fire.

I had dated quite a bit in high school and college and had gotten pinned (pre-engaged) to my college boyfriend my senior year. We were quite serious, dating for four years, including two years after college. Having been raised Catholic, I managed to put off the big deed with all my boyfriends up until then, assuaging the guilt of any goofing around by never quite getting to home run territory with any of them. While my parents neglected to have a big talk with me about the birds and the bees, the unspoken message was clear: no sex before marriage. Period. My college beau was my first, a decision we made slowly and thoughtfully.

After we went our separate ways, I dated several more guys, and while I did have sex with one before Andrew, it was along the lines of what I considered surprise sex, which meant I never actually prepared for it because I wasn't planning to do it. Somehow, in my crazy, Catholic, morality-driven mind, if I used birth control, I would be planning to have sex. At age twenty-four, it seemed better to pretend I wouldn't be having sex than to prepare just in case—as though God was really not going to know the difference. Besides, getting pregnant wasn't part of my plan for a long time. Flawed thinking, yes, but I could live with myself—and my guilty conscience. I'll be the first to admit that for such a smart young woman, this line of thought didn't make much sense.

Andrew and I had surprise sex more than once after a few months. I would always feel guilty afterward and swear it wouldn't happen again, but, of course, it did. I have no excuse for my stupidity, except that it was drilled into my head that you JUST SAID NO to sex before marriage and no one said the rules changed even if you were a healthy young adult in a relationship. I even had a diaphragm from my earlier days, but I wouldn't use it until the last minute, if at all. And this was before the AIDS/STD crisis, so condoms weren't a regular practice. After we'd been dating for a while and things were going really well with Andrew, I decided I would start using the diaphragm regularly.

Too little, too late. That February, I never got my period.

expecting the
unexpected

"Please, please, please . . ." I whispered to myself as I sat on the toilet with the pregnancy test wand in my hand, waiting and praying not to see a plus sign. I was almost a month late, and it had been the longest month of my life. Back in 1981, there was no four-days-late test. You waited WEEKS, wondering if your entire world was going to explode, coming up with excuse after excuse for why this period might be late.

As I sat there, my head spinning with what-ifs and self-recrimination, there was still that twenty-four-year-old part of my brain that knew there was no way this could actually happen to me. This just wouldn't happen. I clung to that hope as I focused on the small screen that remained blank for the moment. *What an idiot you are*, I silently reprimanded myself. *If this is negative, please, God, I will NEVER take a chance like this again.* The irony was not lost on me that I'd been so very careful with my college boyfriend of four years, who I was pretty sure I was going to marry, and now ridiculously not careful with some-one I'd dated for less than four months.

"Please don't be positive," I begged. "I swear I will never have sex again." These promises faded away as the image began to appear on the wand and a tiny plus sign began to materialize. I stared at it in horror, and it seemed like the bottom of my stomach just fell out. The voices in my head were strangely silent, and, in fact, everything became absolutely still, focused on that smallest of plus signs. I had not one thought. I was so shocked, in such disbelief, that no emotions surged to the surface. I was stunned into a literal daze.

That didn't last long. I got up and went into my bedroom and curled up in a ball. When I was a baby, I used to bang my head on my crib before falling asleep. This slightly disturbing phenomenon gave way as a child to rolling back and forth in bed to put myself to sleep, and eventually it stopped altogether. As I lay in bed under the weight of this implausible news, the long-gone self-soothing method came instinctively back, and I began to roll back and forth. I have no idea how much time passed. After a while, as the reality began to sink in, I stopped rolling. The thoughts that had come to a standstill earlier began to fly around in my head like the wicked witch's monkeys.

"What am I going to do?" I asked myself out loud. The enormity of the situation became overwhelming. If you've never been in this state, it's hard to explain the fear, anguish, and terror that come over you. The funny thing is, at that moment, I just knew it was true. I didn't feel the need to run out and buy ten more pregnancy tests. I didn't experience the disbelief many feel. Once I saw that plus sign, it became my truth, maybe because I suddenly acknowledged the small indicators that I'd noticed but dismissed.

I remember feeling very alone that night. I had lots of friends and was very close to my family, but in no way was I prepared to start bringing people into this alternate universe with me. There was only one person I needed to tell right away, and it wasn't going to be easy. I dreaded that about as much as I had dreaded taking the pregnancy test. Here I was, pregnant with his baby, and I didn't even know him well enough to know how he would react. There wasn't a lot of sleep that night.

The next morning, I woke up after having finally passed out sometime before dawn. For a merciful few seconds, I had that blissful unburdened feeling that one experiences upon awakening before reality comes crashing back. And then it came. "I'm pregnant," I muttered, falling back on the pillow. "I am going to have a baby." That was absolutely the most ridiculous sentence I could imagine.

Somehow, I had to just get myself through that day at work. I'm sure I was like a zombie on autopilot, but, honestly, I have no recollection of how I even got anything accomplished. I was just biding time, waiting until the moment Andrew came over after work and I was going to have to tell him. I was feeling sorry for him. He was blithely expecting to go out for another carefree, light-hearted dinner with no worries more difficult than what kind of food to eat or what kind of wine to order. *I'm actually a little envious of him: not knowing, not a care in the world,* I thought to myself. *I wish I didn't have to ruin that for him.*

The clock ticked by almost as if in slow motion. And then I was walking home, and with each step, my stomach got a little queasier, and not from morning sickness. This was going to be one of the hardest things I'd ever had to do. As terrible as it was to be alone with the knowledge that my life would never be the same, it was worse to inflict that fate on someone else. Plus, it was another step toward making this whole thing very, very real.

Andrew called to say he was on his way moments after I put my purse on the counter and took my shoes off. "O Lord," I prayed, "I'm going to need some help with this. I have no idea how to even start this conversation." I went into the bathroom to freshen up and found myself automatically checking to see if I'd started my period. I looked at myself in the mirror. *Guess you don't have to do that anymore,* I thought, and felt the tears start welling up. "Stop it!" I scolded myself. "Snap out of it; you have to hold it together." After a few minor repairs to my makeup, the buzzer sounded to tell me Andrew was downstairs. Resolute eyes stared back at me. "This is it," I said to no one.

Andrew sat on my couch staring blankly at me. I sat across from him, just waiting for him to say something.

"Are you sure?" he finally said. "How is this possible? We haven't even had sex that much!"

I looked at him wryly. We both knew it took only once, and besides, it wasn't like we'd taken foolproof precautions, but I understood—it still seemed impossible.

"You said you were late, but you seemed so sure there was no way," he pleaded.

"I believed that," I said quietly. "I guess I was wrong."

He sat quietly for a minute, trying to absorb this. I knew exactly how he felt, and it wasn't pleasant. At least he wasn't angry, screaming at me. He seemed almost analytical about it.

"So you're sure," he repeated. "You've been to a doctor?"

"No," I said. "But I took a pregnancy test and it was positive."

His eyes lit up.

"Then there's a chance it's not true!" he exclaimed. "Those tests sometimes have false results!"

I considered this. On the one hand, I'd had some of the signs I'd heard about . . . breast tenderness, fatigue . . . so I just assumed it was true. But Andrew worked in medical sales and probably knew more about this stuff. And some of those symptoms happened anyway sometimes. *What if . . . ?* I stared at Andrew and then bolted out the front door.

I walked out of the bathroom with dread written all over my face. All of the hopeful euphoria I'd been feeling in the last hour had drained away when that stupid little plus sign appeared on the just-purchased second pregnancy test wand. Andrew sat there waiting, and I watched his face mirror everything I felt. I slowly sank down next to him on the couch.

"Holy shit," he intoned. "So that's it. I guess you need to see a doctor to know for sure, but two in a row changes the odds."

I was slumped down in the cushions. "It's true," I said morosely. "I knew it. I don't know why I thought any differently."

A few seconds passed, and then Andrew said quietly, "Now what?"

I knew what he was asking, and, strangely, I hadn't thought past the revelation that I was pregnant. But there was no question, not even for an instant. An abortion was not part of the equation for me. I had made my choice when I decided to have sex, even though I hadn't thoughtfully, or maturely, made the decision. I believed we had created a living being, and besides, that was just not something I could ever do. I was having this baby, but what happened after that was a big question mark.

"I'm having the baby, Andrew," I said half out loud. "Abortion is not an option." *There . . . I said it.* Now we were another step up on the ladder to an unknown future.

Andrew paused and, to his credit, never once questioned it or tried to swing it in another direction. I will always be grateful to him that I didn't have to even discuss the issue. There were way too many other things to discuss.

"It seemed like we were so careful," he murmured, and I could see he was going through all the stages I'd gone through the night before.

"Not always," I said. "And, anyway, not careful enough, I guess." I could see in his face that all kinds of things were going on in his head—shock, anger, denial. If we'd been dating for years, or if it was decades later, when pregnancy before marriage was more acceptable, our conversation might have been different. But instead, the two of us sat there, shell-shocked and quiet . . . waiting for someone else to say something. This was a life changer, and neither one of us even knew if the other was *the one*, let alone the one with whom we wanted to parent a child. This was way too soon.

"Okay," he finally said. "So if you're having the baby . . . then what? How do we handle this? What choices do we have?" Like I knew.

I answered quickly, having given it no thought whatsoever. "I'm not ready to get married," I said emphatically. Something flickered across his face . . . relief? I continued, "I don't want to get married because I'm having a baby; I want it to be because it's the right thing to do. But I don't know if I can do this alone. I need to take the time to figure things out."

Where was this all coming from? I sounded like I'd given this careful consideration and had a confident game plan. This was absurd. Inside, it was as though my brain neurons were exploding with messages . . . questions, fears, hopes, possible solutions. Nothing was clear cut; nothing was absolute.

Andrew looked at me carefully, and then he did exactly the right thing. He reached over and pulled me into his arms. "We'll figure it out," he said. I felt a little better, although I wondered just how we might do that. At least it didn't seem like he was going to walk out of my life and leave me to face this alone. That in itself was a relief.

secret lives

As the next few weeks passed, it never really got easier, but the reality wove itself into the fabric of my everyday life. Andrew told me he intended to be there for me—he would not abandon me to handle this on my own, but that was the extent of what he could commit to at this time, and I was fine with that. I dealt with the problem of telling friends, family, and work by not telling anyone. There was no reason to jump in with both feet prematurely, I told myself, especially when I knew for a fact it was going to be very icy water. So I buried myself in my job, even during the periods when I could barely keep my eyes open from fatigue. I would want to crawl under my desk, craving just a few minutes for a short nap, and then berate myself for the thought. *Yeah, that's a great idea,* I'd think with a snort. *No one will be suspicious if they find you asleep under the desk.* And I'd muster the energy somehow to get through the day, only to crash at night.

It was through my job that I picked an additional co-conspirator: my obstetrician. Since this was a completely foreign area for me (I "wasn't having sex," so I didn't even have a gynecologist in Chicago), I was at a loss as to how you chose a doctor. Then it dawned on me that I had booked a wonderful, kind, personable doctor from the Chicago area for a show recently . . . a man who had modern, pro-female inclinations and was an expert in all things concerning reproduction. The only downside was that his office was forty-five minutes outside of town and his affiliated hospital was an hour away. Still, I trusted him and felt that in these difficult circumstances, I could be honest with him, and that counted for a lot.

Andrew took me to the first appointment and sat in the waiting room while Dr. Morgan confirmed to me what we already knew. I was started on prenatal vitamins and told what to expect during the pregnancy. When I told Dr. Morgan that I wasn't sure what would happen after the baby was born, he hugged me. "I am here for you, and I will help in any way I can," he assured me. In that moment, I knew he was the right doctor for the job.

On the drive home, Andrew and I didn't talk much. We both were in our own worlds, having had official verification of our predicament. We could no longer pretend that maybe, just maybe, I had an ovarian cyst or endometriosis or something besides being pregnant. This was real, and although we'd been agonizing over it for the last couple weeks, the doctor's visit made it all the more concrete. It was daunting.

We spent a lot of time together through those nights that followed. We'd get takeout while I sprawled on the couch. We would watch movies at home and spend most of the time talking about anything but the obvious problem. I never got sick, but a lot of foods just didn't appeal to me, and instead of gaining weight, I lost weight for the first few months, so it was easy to not look pregnant. But pregnant I was, and it weighed on my mind heavily and constantly.

I was determined that Andrew not feel pressured into marriage, and I also didn't want to marry the wrong guy because I was pregnant. But I didn't know if Andrew was the right or wrong guy. The more time we spent together, the more comfortable we were. And although he could be evasive and distant, especially when the subject of the baby came up, he could also be loving and fun. I was utterly at a loss as to how to proceed. After all, if he *was* the right one, then having the baby might be putting the horse before the cart, but whatever; worse things happened. If he wasn't, could I do this on my own? All alone, in a city with no support system? My head was cluttered with ifs, buts, pros, and cons. It was time to at least bring in another viewpoint.

I sat listening to my mom talk about her latest tennis match and the trip she and my dad were planning. *Should I just interrupt her? Maybe tell her to put Daddy on the phone?* I could not for the life of me figure out the best way to say what I had to say. I probably should have driven the five hours home to tell them, but there didn't seem to be a good weekend for that, and I didn't have an infinite amount of time. Finally, I just burst in on her.

"Mom, I have to tell you something!" I interrupted, immediately wishing I could push rewind. What an original opening.

Big pause. (Now that I'm a parent, I know those are words no parent wants to hear.) "Is Dad home?" I asked tentatively.

"Sure . . . let me get him on the extension," she said hesitantly. One minute—that minute could have lasted a month as far as I was concerned—passed before I heard my mom say, "Okay, we're both here."

Oh, geez; this was it. How to explain? How to break the news that I wasn't the sainted, virginal daughter they thought I was? "Ummm, well, I . . . uh, I'm not sure . . ." I stammered into the phone, completely dumbstruck. This was harder than I thought, perhaps harder than telling Andrew. On second thought, not as hard as that. I took a deep breath.

"Lorri, what is it?" my mom asked with some urgency. "You're scaring us. What, are you pregnant or something?"

I almost dropped the phone. "Well, um, actually, I, um . . . I am," I finally got out.

There was pretty much silence on the other end.

"Really?" my mom finally squeaked. "Are you serious?"

"Very serious," I answered, "and very upset." I didn't get the reaction I was expecting. My mom had no judgment for me. She actually set about comforting me, getting details, asking questions. Had I seen a doctor, what was Andrew's response, did I know what I was going to do, what did my boss say? I couldn't believe how well they were taking it. My mom felt so bad for me and worried what would happen with my practically new job.

My dad didn't say much; in fact, he was quiet most of the conversation. Finally, I couldn't stand it anymore. "Dad, I'm sorry about this. I'm sure you're disappointed."

That's when he said, "Lorri, I never expected you to be celibate, but I expected you to be smart."

You could have heard a pin drop across the phone line. I felt like the air got sucked out of the room.

Those words will stick with me as long as I live. They reverberated in my head. They became the punch line of the birds-and-bees lessons I gave my girls years later, using my story as an example of what could happen. Why hadn't someone mentioned that to me somewhere along the way? He didn't expect me to be celibate? I expected me to be celibate! I expected it so much that rather than NOT be celibate, I opted to not prepare and to pretend that it wasn't going to happen!

"WHAT?" I asked incredulously. "Why didn't anyone say something like that? No one ever mentioned there was an expiration date on 'no sex before marriage'!"

"C'mon, Lorri," he said. "You're twenty-four years old—you're an adult!"

I sat quietly while my dad's words washed over me. I was an adult with an adult's problem. This was for me to figure out, not my parents. I could see that they would be supportive of whatever decision I made, but it was my decision.

Now my family knew, but Andrew had no intention of telling his family. Or anyone, for that matter. After a couple of months, when I started to feel energetic again, we made plans to see some very close friends of his, and we were also scheduled to go to his parents' house for a family event.

"I don't want you to say anything to anyone," he warned me.

I looked at him quizzically. "What do you mean?" I probed, "Like, ever?" There was an evasiveness about him that I didn't like. And what happened when one day I showed up with a baby?

"Well, you're not showing, and we don't know what's going to happen," he explained. "There's no reason to get a bunch of people involved, and I don't want my family putting any pressure on us or giving us opinions. Let's just go have fun and not talk about it," he finished quickly.

"I'm not sure not talking about it is the answer," I muttered, but Andrew was adamant. If I wanted my family and friends to know, that was my business, but mum was the word as far as anybody on his side. We were socially active and saw his connections quite regularly, and all they really knew about me after that was that I did not wear fitted clothing.

I have always been something of an open book, and there was no way I would be able to, or want to, keep the lid on this. I needed to bounce ideas off someone besides Andrew, who often avoided the subject. I told some close friends, and then it was time to tell my boss, Phil, and my supervisor, Wendy. I was sure to pop out any minute, and I had to let them know before that happened. This moment was right up there with telling Andrew and my parents. What if they decided the best solution was to fire me? I hadn't even been there a year—what kind of loyalty could they possibly owe me?

I needn't have worried. I forgot whom I worked for: Phil Donahue, who fought for women's rights and looked out for people who needed help. Phil's good friends were the top feminists of the day: Gloria Steinem, Betty Friedan, and, yes, Marlo Thomas—his wife. The same Marlo who had starred in the 1960s groundbreaking sitcom *That Girl*, about a single woman in the working world. Ironic. Having Phil Donahue in my corner was like being Rocky Balboa with coach Mickey Goldmill in the ring with him, and firing a woman because she was pregnant would be the last thing Phil would do.

I found myself telling Phil and Wendy much more than I intended. I meant to just go in, state the facts, and tell them my work would not be affected. Who was I kidding? Phil was the best interviewer on television; he could get even the most reluctant guest to talk. Before I knew it, the whole story was out there, and Phil was offering to help in any way he could.

"You don't have to make any decisions yet," he assured me. "You have time, and you need to really think this through. Just know your job is secure, and we are here for you." I could have kissed him. With everything going on, it was such a relief to know that at least my job was safe and I wasn't going to end up on the street.

It was mid-summer, and I really wasn't that much closer to a decision on what would happen when the inevitable occurred. Andrew and I had kind of been carrying on with business as usual, and without much of a baby bump, it was sometimes almost possible to forget what we were facing. I was starting to get little reminders, though, in the form of flutters and slight movements, and as I entered my sixth month, it became hard to disguise what was going on under my fashionable sundresses. We had weekend plans to go up to Wisconsin to see Andrew's family when he suggested we sit down for a minute.

"I've been thinking," he started, and I immediately snapped to attention. What was this? Was he starting to realize what I was realizing, that we were really getting along and perhaps we should start discussing the possibility of a future? He hemmed and hawed a little and then said, "I don't think you should come with me this weekend. I think it's starting to become obvious that you're pregnant."

I stared at him, not quite believing the words I was hearing. "So, what do you mean?" I ventured. "Are you saying that now that I'm showing, we're still not going to tell anyone we know? I'm just going to disappear?"

Andrew looked down. It seemed he didn't really want to look me in the eye. "I told you I didn't want anyone I knew to know," he said carefully. "The only way we can do that now is if they don't see you. I'll make excuses for you." Boy, was I on the wrong track! Considering a future was the last thing on his mind. He was trying to figure out how to keep me in the closet—forever, if necessary. All I knew was that this was one mind-blowing secret, and the first thing that popped into my mind was "Oh, what a tangled web we weave, when first we practice to deceive."

I said nothing, though. I was hurt and disappointed, and something inside me broke. Option number 1, staying together and raising this baby, was not looking so good.

CHAPTER FIVE

pros and cons

Now that the evidence was out there for everyone to see, I needed to bite the bullet and just admit what was going on to curious friends and acquaintances, especially at work. I filled in the awkward pauses when it was clear people were wondering how to ask about the obvious. What was amazing to me was how many people either knew someone who had been in or had themselves been in similar unexpected circumstances. It was like so many life experiences that people don't talk about, but as soon as you do, you find out everyone has a skeleton in their closet. People started confiding in me about the time they had gotten pregnant, or their girlfriend, or a sister, or an aunt. It became clear that I wasn't alone in this predicament; it was just that no one ever spoke casually about it.

Especially because the vast majority had had abortions. They never spoke about it, because it never became an issue, until a haunting reminder like me came along. And if they kept the baby, they often married and went on with their lives; they didn't talk about getting pregnant accidentally. People were incredibly curious about what I was going to do and how I would manage in the end. "But what will you do when the baby comes?" the woman I barely knew in the mailroom asked inquisitively. I just shook my head and gave the answer I'd manufactured after being asked the same question a few times.

"I'll figure it out," I said with false confidence. "I'll either keep the baby, or there's also adoption."

I got ready for the usual response, and sure enough, there it was. "Adoption! Are you really going to be able to give up that baby after carrying it for nine months?" Good grief, how did I know? And how did people have the nerve to ask me that? And then came the statement that shocked me to the core.

"I could never do that," the woman confessed. "I accidentally got pregnant three times and had abortions." I just stared at her. "I could never bear to give up a baby for adoption," she finished. I mumbled something about having to get back to work and hurried down the hall. When I got back to the office, I closed my door, sat in the chair, and put my head in my hands, thinking about the conversation.

First, let's not even talk about the three times . . . that was inconceivable to me. I couldn't understand how ending a baby's life was easier than giving him or her a chance at life. Being in this situation, I certainly saw where you might feel helpless or without options. I absolutely understood the desperation, the feeling that you were alone and in an impossible situation. And I understood the temptation to end the problem before anyone knew about it. But with so many people wanting babies, why wouldn't you want to give your own baby a chance to live, even if you couldn't raise him or her yourself?

Which brought me to the second, and equally disturbing, point I'd taken from the brief talk with the mailroom lady. When mulling over possible options for myself, adoption was always thrown in as one of the potential outcomes. *What do I actually know about adoption?* I asked myself now. *If it's easier to have an abortion, how hard is adoption going to be? Will I be able to do that?* It was a wake-up call that all of my alternatives were going to be difficult, no matter what I chose.

Actually, I hadn't really thought through the logistics of my adoption option. I guess I'd been focused on the possibility that Andrew would miraculously turn out to be Mr. Right and we'd have a happily-ever-after solution to our immediate problem. While a part of me still hung on to that prospect, I knew I had to begin to seriously consider the idea of adoption and do more than just end my standard answer to questions with ". . . and adoption." I needed to get educated, and even thinking about it, with my hand on my expanding belly, brought tears to my eyes.

The way I saw it, there were three possible outcomes. Now that the shock had worn off and the baby was a physical presence, I was forced to think through to that tenth month. Door number one involved Andrew and me realizing that we were, in fact, soul mates and that our love child was just that . . . a product of a love meant to be. The second door assumed the opposite, that Andrew and I were not supposed to be together and that I would now raise this child by myself. And door number three was the adoption door: a choice that devastated me but would give the baby a chance at a complete life with a devoted mom and dad—and this door would give a couple the best gift of their lives.

I began to do what I knew best . . . research. I started on a national level and worked my way to local Chicago sources. I spoke to experts in the field and providers all over the country. I was surprised to learn that one of the longest-running and most well-respected agencies was right in Evanston, Illinois, just north of Chicago!

I dialed the phone number of The Cradle, stated my case, and was quickly transferred to a reassuring woman who calmly explained how an adoption would evolve. After hearing about the process and asking a few more questions, I felt like I had a handle on what would need to be done and when. Instead of moving into a hard-sell position, the woman said in a nurturing tone, "Take your time deciding. You still have a few months, and this has got to be the biggest decision of your life. We are here for you, and we're not going anywhere." I hung up the phone feeling a teeny, tiny bit better but no closer to a decision.

I sat there, once again agonizing over how I was going to choose my fate and that of this tiny life inside me. Adoption remained door number three, the last of my three choices, as I went over to Andrew's that night and told him about my conversation with The Cradle.

"Well, that sounds like a great place," he said carefully. "That could be a really good solution."

"Really?" I asked dryly. "I just feel like at twenty-four, I should not be putting my baby up for adoption. As an adult, I should be able to figure this out without resorting to that."

He looked down at his folded hands, his elbows on his knees. "I don't know if that's true," he replied. "I mean, we were so new in our relationship when this happened, and now we have this stressful pressure on us. We haven't really had time to just be us and see if we're right for each other."

I nodded slowly. All that was true. "But we don't have the luxury of the normal progression of a relationship. It's not going to happen. We just have to figure this out, and we have a deadline, unfortunately."

"I just don't see it that way," Andrew said analytically. "Look, I'm going to be here for you through the pregnancy and the delivery. I'm not going to disappear. We're partners in this. But I think we should first get through this and then see where our relationship goes."

"Get through this?" I repeated. "A baby isn't something you just get through! What if we stay together? We'll have given up our child!"

Andrew shook his head. "I don't know," he said abruptly. "We're in crisis mode. I don't see how we can figure it all out in three months."

And he walked into the kitchen. Conversation over.

CHAPTER SIX

i feel you

The bump was growing. And moving. And kicking. At work, I often found myself with my hand across my belly, rubbing the sharp little edges that were noticeably pushing from the inside. *Donahue* guests would smile and say "Congratulations" or cheerfully ask me, "When are you due?" I was under no obligation to explain that this wasn't your ordinary pregnancy because I would never see them again, so I would just smile and play along. There were times when I could almost forget that I had a special kind of drama playing out or that my due date was actually something I was dreading. As long as there wasn't an actual baby present, I could pretend there was nothing wrong.

During this time, there was a definite shift in my thinking toward the pregnancy. Suddenly, it was no longer *the* baby; it was now *my* baby. There was a relationship developing between this baby and me, this baby who had appeared, unbidden and unexpectedly, inside of me. I definitely cared deeply about what would happen to my child, and I began to be very curious about what size he or she was and whom he or she might look like. I would usually catch myself before letting the fantasy get too far, but I couldn't stop the love I felt.

"Do you want to know?" Dr. Morgan asked during a routine visit. We were discussing an amniocentesis, the only sure way to find out if I was having a boy or girl. While he was definitely against unnecessary testing, many people were opting to take the diagnostic test, which had the side benefit of determining the sex. Ultrasounds were nothing like the 3D and 4D tests of today, and Dr. Morgan did not believe in doing a whole bunch of tests just for fun, especially an amnio, which did have certain inherent risks.

"No," I answered in a small voice. "We still don't know what we're going to do, and knowing the sex would just make it harder. I would start visualizing more, and . . ." my voice trailed off.

"Say no more," he said gently. "I'd rather not do it anyway, so there's nothing to worry about." I loved this man.

But not knowing the gender really didn't make anything easier. It certainly didn't make me care less. At work, I buried myself in the show, and I began to feel like an average expectant working mother most of the time. We had plenty to keep us busy, and there was no need for small talk about what had already been discussed, so we just went about our business. My work life was pretty normal—considering I was facing a monumental calamity in my near future.

But once I got home each evening, it was different. I'd sit on the couch and feel the elbows and feet pushing around. I read the usual books to prepare for labor and delivery—which was terrifying. I grew to love the unknown person inside of me, despite efforts to not get too close. I didn't know what the future held. I played music close to my belly, made sure I was eating and drinking good foods for the baby's development, and talked to my baby. I even wrote poems, such as this one:

BABY

Baby, I feel you.
I'm starting to see you.
I want to love you.
My childlike innocence has created a child.
Now I know better, but
The cost of this lesson is you.

Andrew, on the other hand, compartmentalized us. He would take me to the doctor appointments almost an hour away. He was attentive to my needs and even felt the baby move every now and then. There were times when I thought, *Wait a minute; I think he's getting it; I think he's feeling it too,* and then he'd put the wall back up.

The two of us were getting along incredibly well, in spite of this bizarre barrier. I had energy and felt great, and with my job, we had our choice of entertainment options. We went to movie premieres, book signing events, and office parties. We went to great restaurants and celebrated special occasions. We were together almost all the time after work, and we laughed a lot, which says something under the circumstances. Somehow, though, while I was ready to consider all of this, including the fact that a baby was at stake, he was not. We would be talking, or laughing, or making love, and I would begin to wonder why we had to wait to "get through this." I would think, *This is great! Why can't we explore now whether or not we belong together, because if we do, let's do this and be a family.*

But Andrew seemed to be stuck in time. He was so afraid to commit to marriage just because there was a baby that he refused to admit anything at all. It was as though we were hovering in space. Our relationship deepened, and we really got to know each other, but there was no getting to the next level like one would in a normal situation. We remained in limbo, and he didn't seem to understand that he stood to lose a son or a daughter. In his mind, it seemed that our November due date was going to be the day our crisis ended and normal life resumed. In my mind, I knew that would be when the crisis began.

It was so strange how different our perspectives were, because it was clear we both cared about each other. He was anxious for the day when he could pretend it never happened, we could resume socializing with his friends and family, and our relationship could then progress or not progress just like any other couple. I, on the other hand, feared that day and knew it would change everything. If Andrew didn't come around and realize what was at stake, I couldn't see past that day. I had to deal with facts, and I'd either lose my baby through adoption or lose my life as I knew it by becoming a single mother. I couldn't count on Andrew to have an epiphany later. I could count only on being alone. Without realizing it, deep inside my subconscious, I think I began to build my own walls. They were invisible, and it's only in retrospect that I can see that this must have happened. It became the baby and me against Andrew.

the most difficult decision

It was hard to decide what college to attend. It was hard to decide to leave a sure job and become a ski bum. It was also hard to decide where to move to start my career. Those decisions were mere child's play, however, compared to what I was facing now. The bigger the baby got, the more horrendous the evaluation process became. I was choosing what this child's future was going to be. What I decided would set the baby's course. I felt like Atlas, with the weight of this on my shoulders.

There were many factors, but not many facts. I instinctively turned to what I knew—troubleshooting and finding answers. Working with Phil taught me to not take no for an answer, to keep digging until you reach the goal. I had to be sure I had gathered all the relevant information in order to make a truly informed decision. I began talking to friends with children and figured out quickly that if I kept the baby, I would need a support system. Staying in Chicago would be difficult, if not impossible. My job was 24/7, including nights and weekends. A regular daycare would not cut it. My salary would not afford me the luxury of a full-time nanny, and without family near, I would spend every extra penny on childcare and most of my hours at work.

So I considered giving up my incredible, amazing job. I thought long and hard about options. *What if I moved back to the Dayton area,* I'd think, *or maybe the Cincinnati area? What could I do for work if I moved closer to my family?* This was a discouraging line of thought. I'd left Dayton before, when I moved to Colorado. Yes, I was in search of an adventure then, but there was also not much in the way of television production jobs there.

It made me sad to think about leaving Chicago, my job, and Andrew. But this option allowed me to keep the baby, so I contacted old friends in Ohio and asked about the cost of living, the price of housing, the opportunities. I called around the area to inquire about television jobs. Every one of them was incredulous that I would consider leaving my job at *Donahue*. I talked to my family, and while I deduced that my parents were not going to be childcare providers, they were very clear to say they would support any decision I made. But, doing the math, and even taking into consideration the cost of living variables, I could see that my baby would end up in daycare, I would end up at a lower-paying job, and my career path would take a definite dive. I'd be raising my baby alone, albeit with family close by, and at age 25, I'd be worse off than I was three years earlier. And I'd be in Dayton instead of Chicago.

Option two, keeping the baby to raise alone, was a sad picture for both me and this precious child I loved. Hours, days, years in daycare, with our time together being some nights and weekends. Not the life I wanted for my child. Yet this option was one that didn't feel like a knife in my heart.

Option three, adoption, broke my heart just thinking about it. It probably made the most sense for the baby—two doting and completely devoted full-time parents. It had the added benefit of being a tremendous gift to a committed couple, desperate to have a family. It would be win-win for the three of them, but a definite loss for me. Yes, I would stay in Chicago and keep my job. This option would affect my life the least—other than to completely devastate me emotionally.

And option one was fast disappearing. It had become clear that Andrew was not going to figure out his feelings about me until the baby was no longer in the picture. He never told me what to do or gave his opinion outright, but the message was unmistakably there in everything he said and didn't say. Adoption was his choice. Adoption was the answer for him. There was not going to be a happily ever after for the three of us.

Suddenly, there was an option four. My married sister, Kim, who lived in Dayton near my parents, called me one weekend with an offer.

"What if Chuck and I adopted your baby?" she asked.

I was sure I hadn't heard her correctly. "You what?" I squeaked.

"We would like you to consider letting us adopt your baby," she repeated.

For a minute, my heart began to race, and I felt a hopeful jolt of electricity run through my body. *What an idea,* I thought, still not saying anything out loud. *She has three kids, so my baby would be part of a family . . . my family . . . I could see him . . . I'd know everything about her . . .*

My thoughts all ran together until my sister interrupted, "So, what do you think?" What did I think? I had hope! I . . . now other thoughts started to crowd in. *She has three kids . . . how could she possibly love my baby like she loves hers? Their marriage isn't that great . . . what if they got divorced . . . what would happen to my child . . . what if I didn't approve of how she parented . . . ?* Before I could speak, I'd already become the devil's advocate, and both sides of the question lay before me.

"I think," I began quietly, "that this is an amazing offer. So generous, so sweet. I love you for suggesting it. I never thought about this, and I think I need to think it through."

She paused and then said, "Well, there's one more thing." I waited, wondering what more she could possibly add.

"We've discussed this, and the only way we could do this is if you promised that the baby would be ours," she said solemnly. "It would not be on loan to us, you could not be involved in raising it, and you could not question our decisions regarding it."

I swallowed hard. "That makes perfect sense," I whispered. "I completely understand that part of it." After thanking her again for even making the overture, I hung up the phone. I had a lot to think about.

a heart-wrenching dialogue

Time was running out, and I was no closer to a decision than I had been seven months ago. Andrew was slouching on the couch next to me when I told him about my sister's offer. He sat straight up and turned to look at me.

"What do you think about that idea?" he asked carefully. Just looking at him, I could see he wasn't crazy about the notion.

"I'm not sure," I responded honestly. "I would love to know where the baby was, and it would be so great to be able to watch him or her grow up."

"I don't know," he replied. "Don't you think it would be hard to know where he or she lived . . . to see your sister raising your child? And I thought she and her husband weren't getting along," he added.

"Yeah, I thought about that. It's definitely not a perfect scenario." I glossed over the fact that Andrew just called *our* baby "your child." He had just voiced some of my objections to the idea, and I had quite a few more, especially the worry that I couldn't interfere no matter what, even if I took issue with parenting or circumstances. I loved my sister, but she and her husband definitely had issues and concerns that gave me pause.

I decided to talk to my parents and get their input on the idea. While they shared my gratitude that she had been bighearted enough to make the proposition, they also saw flaws in the plan, and as parents, they worried that if anything were to go wrong, it could end up dividing the family. In the end, I decided to take option four off the table. There were too many questionable variables and a potential for disaster. When I told my sister, she didn't seem surprised.

"I knew it wasn't a picture-perfect plan," she admitted. "But we were willing to do it, and still are, if you change your mind. I just didn't want to see you lose the baby. I've had children, and I couldn't bear the thought of you giving your child to strangers. I wanted to try to keep it in the family."

I started to cry, especially at the "stranger" reference. "I can't bear it either… I have no good choices," I sobbed. "There is no clear-cut answer for me." When I hung up the phone, I was back down to three possible scenarios— two, really. It had been some time since Andrew and I had even discussed the impending birth. He just didn't want to talk about it. There was no doubt in my mind that he had made his decision, but that didn't stop me from hoping. The baby was now a constant presence in my life, literally. The movements, kicking, and rolling around were miracles to me. I could practically see the tiny shape all crammed up inside. If Andrew made one overture to say he wanted to be together, I knew instinctively that I would marry him whether he was Mr. Right or not. If I could just keep this little being, who was assertively letting me know he or she was in there, I was sure I could make the relationship work. Just as Andrew chose to do nothing, I chose to ignore his distance: the detachment, the reserve that bordered on coldness when things got too close. I think I moved forward towards adoption one baby step at a time while subconsciously clinging to the chance that he would feel the baby's movement or see my swollen belly, slap himself on the forehead, and admit what a fool he'd been.

My time at home and with Andrew seemed to point me toward adoption, but meanwhile, my office colleagues and friends were trying to steer me in the other direction. As we inched toward my due date, everyone had an opinion, as though time was running out, which, of course, it was. Friends would call to see how I was doing and then ask questions like "Can't you just try to make it work with Andrew?" or "Won't your parents help you?" I couldn't blame them for their curiosity. There was no way they could understand all the complications of what I was going through or realize my state of mind.

Every time I was at a *Donahue* event or over at the main office, my coworkers tried their best to be in my corner while trying to convince me that I could do this alone. They didn't want to interfere, but so many thought I should keep the baby. My boss, Phil, even subtly dropped hints that I could bring the baby to work with me, and I'd grasp onto that idea even while knowing how unworkable that would be. I could not picture how I could talk to a guest in the green room with a baby on my hip. I just didn't have a "bring your baby to work" kind of job or a job that I could do from home. But, to give him credit, he was trying to offer a solution that was not done back in 1981. People didn't set up port-a-cribs in their offices or take breastfeeding breaks. Bosses like Phil were nonexistent thirty years ago and are still rare today.

I tried to avoid the inevitable. I went to work, I came home, and Andrew and I spent time together, but we didn't talk much about the baby anymore. I felt sure that Andrew's decision was made, and I began to lean toward adoption, too. I had major doubts about our relationship at this point. I was alone in a big city, and I had a very demanding job. *How can I do this by myself?* I would ask myself. *If I do, is this really the best life for my baby?* This baby's welfare was at the top of my list, as I would stroke my stomach and feel the strong responses.

One night, I told Andrew I had decided to go to Lamaze classes.

After a noticeable pause, he said, "Okay, I'll go with you." This man was full of surprises.

"Um, that's great," I said. I had been prepared to launch into a detailed explanation about why it was important to be prepared for what was ahead and was ready for his excuses for not being able to go with me. But no—he was willing to do the classes! As it turns out, however, he was not willing to be my birthing coach.

We went to the first class and immediately found ourselves in the awkward position of having to introduce ourselves to the rest of the class: ten or twelve married couples, all deliriously happy, mooning over each other, and excited about what was to come. To my embarrassed ears, our different last names were like neon lights spelling out WE ARE NOT MARRIED. Next was the movie of the live birth, which terrified both Andrew and me. Neither one of us had any knowledge whatsoever of what birthing a baby actually entailed. We would have sat there with our mouths hanging open if we weren't trying so hard to not draw attention to ourselves.

We learned about different types of breathing during labor and then sat on the floor to practice. Andrew sat behind me, and I sat between his legs, following the teacher's instructions. I could almost imagine we were just like the other expectant parents there. There was a lot of talk about what was happening inside my uterus and what the baby looked like at this stage. Andrew was very quiet during all of this, and as I looked at his face, it seemed like all of this was real to him for the first time.

On the way home, I could tell something was heavy on his mind. I was chattering on about something we'd learned when I looked over at him. The shadows of the streetlights played across his face, and I could see the strangely tight expression he wore.

"What's up?" I asked curiously, a little afraid to hear the answer.

He didn't answer immediately but glanced in my direction and then back at the road quickly.

"Uh, I don't know," he started hesitantly. "I guess that class just made me realize a lot of stuff."

My mind began racing, and I felt my stomach tighten. "Like what?" I replied. Was this it? Was he falling for this baby like I was? Did he want to take a chance on us?

"Well," he said slowly, "I don't want you to take this the wrong way, but I don't think I can be the coach when you have the baby."

Take it the wrong way? I was silently crushed. I felt a door slam closed in my head. I sat there and stared out the car window.

"Let me explain," he insisted. "It's not that I don't want to be there. I just don't think I can do it. I can't see this baby. I can't hold this baby." He stopped for a minute, and we drove in silence.

"It isn't that I don't care," he continued after a pause. "It's that I care too much. If I see it, this will all be too hard for me to take. Do you understand that? Do you see that I just can't do this?"

I turned towards him and tried hard to sound calm. "Of course I understand how hard this is," I spit out. "I'm in this too, you know, but I don't have a choice about being there or not being there. There ARE alternatives, though. This doesn't have to be so painful." I was not going to spell it all out and beg him to be a family with us. He was either going to make that decision or not.

"We've already talked about this a million times," he pointed out, as if I didn't know. "We decided adoption is the best answer and that you and I will figure out our relationship after this pregnancy is over."

"YOU decided that," I said, almost under my breath. "I've been willing to keep my options open. Didn't you feel anything in that class? This is a real, live baby we're talking about. It's not so black and white."

His face twisted, and as he pulled the car up in front of my building, he sat staring out into the darkness. "I can't . . . I just can't," he managed to get out. "I can't see the baby. Maybe you and I have a future together, but I can't even think about that right now. This is a crisis we need to get through, and then we can see what happens." He looked miserable and added, "That's what we decided."

I reached for the handle of the car door and got out. "That's what *you* decided," I repeated and then shut the door and walked into the elevator thinking about what just happened. Nothing had really changed, and yet everything had. The Lamaze class had made it crystal clear that we were nearing the end game, and Andrew and I had had opposite reactions to it. On the other hand, he had showed more emotion and distress tonight than ever before. It was apparent that he was covering up a wall of feelings that he refused to admit. It was the first time I had a peek underneath that detached exterior. That night, I went home and wrote another poem.

HE'S HURTING TOO

He's hurting too,
Although who would guess?
His distance and indifference
Have always been his trump card.
But he's hurting too.
Suddenly, all too clear to me,
I see his secret pain, feel the silent tears.
The heart that has seemed invincible
Has been breaking.
Caught in emotion's trap . . .
Jaws, like a noose, tightening
With time's passage.
I thought only I felt the teeth shut on tomorrow's door.
But he felt it. He heard it.
And he's hurting too.

So Andrew was afraid to see the baby. The next day, I called Mariellen, the Lamaze instructor, explained the situation, and asked her if she would consider being my coach. None of my family or friends would have time to go through the classes, and she was a warm, friendly, funny person who happened to be an expert in childbirth. She was an obvious choice, and she readily agreed. I hung up, feeling a bit relieved. Then I picked up the phone again and made the toughest call of my life. I called the adoption agency and made an appointment.

CHAPTER NINE

a nightmare's dream

I sat in my car looking at the beautiful, old stone building with the white rocking chairs on the big porch. *You need to go in there,* I told myself. *You're going to be late.* It was in a lovely part of Evanston, just north of the city, with big, ancient mansions on every block. I had to admit it looked warm and welcoming, not at all like a hole that was going to swallow my baby. Still, I couldn't make myself get out of the car.

About ten minutes went by before I could force myself up to the front door. *This is just an interview,* I coaxed myself. *I'm just going to get some information.* I went through the door and approached the woman at the desk. She smiled cordially, and that gave me the courage to ask for the woman I spoke with on the phone. Before I knew it, I was sitting in front of a kind-looking, sympathetic face.

"It's a pleasure to meet you," Jane said slowly, "and before anything else, please know that you won't be making any decisions today. We are here as a resource for you, and we want to help you through this difficult time. You will make this decision when you are ready, and you won't be alone. We will be with you every step of the way, no matter what you decide to do."

I almost started crying. I realized how alone I'd felt these last months. I may have discussed the situation with different people, but no one had actually gone down this road before. No one knew exactly what I was going through or could understand how I felt, and now, finally, here was someone who did. And she wasn't sitting there rubbing her palms together, plotting how to keep this live one on the line. She cared about me.

Jane and I started talking. We both asked each other a million questions, and her easygoing, compassionate manner set me at ease and allowed me to ask about details I hadn't allowed myself to consider. What would happen to the baby right after birth? How were parents chosen? How much say would I have in the process? Every question was answered thoroughly, and she assured me that I would be an integral part of the process. I would be making all of the decisions. Furthermore, at no time would there be any pressure whatsoever on their part to influence me one way or another.

"It's important that you understand that we consider your welfare to be just as important as the baby's or the adoptive parents'," she insisted. "We are here to support you and carry out *your* wishes."

I filled out a questionnaire about Andrew, my life, my circumstances, and me. When I left several hours later, I had a peace that I hadn't felt in eight months. I felt that if I did make this decision, I had found the right place to make it happen. After talking to Jane, adoption didn't seem like the horrible, heartless thing I'd envisioned. She told me many positive stories and helped me to accept that this choice would be a selfless one.

I waited a few days to tell Andrew that I'd gone to The Cradle. I didn't want to see the relieved expression I knew would pass over his face. He continued to take me to the Lamaze classes, but we didn't bring up the obvious problem that no one wanted to discuss. When I told him The Cradle would like to have his signature as well as mine on a document of relinquishment, he quickly said he would sign it.

I went once or twice a week to see Jane. We discussed how I was feeling and where I was emotionally. I needed to assure her that I knew what I was doing, even though I most certainly did not. At twenty-four years old, I knew I was an unusual birthmother. I was older, not a teen in trouble. I was educated, not a substance abuser. I was in excellent physical and mental health. I was an adoptive parent's dream. Ironic that their dream would be my nightmare.

About two weeks before my due date, Jane told me she had five family profiles for me to read. By this time, I had come to the conclusion that in the real world in which I lived, my baby's best option was adoption. If I still privately struggled emotionally with it, I didn't allow myself to really give in to those feelings anymore. To just about everyone, including myself (most of the time), I had a face of conviction regarding the decision.

Jane handed me a folder. "These are five couples who meet the criteria you gave in your questionnaire. I've been listening to you these past weeks, and I really think any one of these five would be a great fit as far as what you want for your baby."

I had gone through the process of ticking boxes on religion, ethnic background, family dynamics, siblings, extended family, geography, etc. There were lots of basics to weed through, and while I wasn't particular about all, there were a few that mattered: I wanted a Catholic family, I wanted at least one parent to be at home, I did not want the family to have biological children.

If I was going to do this, I was determined that my baby's family was going to be the absolute best family in the world. I didn't ever for one minute allow myself to consider a result like the terrible TV movies and stories of adoptions gone wrong. That was not an option, and I closed my mind to the fact that I could not control the outcome. I could only trust The Cradle to have done a thorough job checking backgrounds and have faith in my own instincts.

Jane left me alone in the room with the file containing the five family profiles. They were very comprehensive, very thorough descriptions of who these people were, why they were looking to adopt, what their professions were, and what they liked to do. It was almost like an out-of-body experience for me . . . I was sitting there reading about people who might soon be holding, loving, and raising my baby. On the one hand, I held their futures in my hands. On the other hand, two of them would hold my child's future. I read through tears, and at one point, the baby kicked inside of me, almost as though I was being told how important this was.

They all sounded wonderful, of course. Each couple had strengths and weaknesses in my eyes, but they were all pretty great: accomplished, loving, intelligent people who were lacking just one ingredient—their own child. One couple, however, stood out. The wife sounded fantastic—she was finishing law school but wanted to be home with their child, when and if they got one. She was a concert-level pianist, she sounded like she had a great sense of humor, and, like me, she and her husband were Roman Catholics. Both of their parents lived close by, so my baby would have grandparents. The husband had a good job, but it sounded like he came from independent means, so providing for my child would not be a problem. One of the most attractive paragraphs, however, pertained to the fact that he himself had been adopted, so at least he intimately understood what it was like, and she had a connection through him.

I left telling Jane I was going to think about it, but I think I knew right away that there was something special about that couple. If I was an adopted child, I would choose them as my parents. Strangely, I became almost methodical in my decision-making. If my emotional self was a three-room house, a whole room had become shuttered: furniture draped and closed up tight. I was absolutely sure that this choice gave my baby the best chance at a good life, and my subconscious shut down the heartbreak, the anxiety, and the sorrow so I could just get through it. All I thought about was a great life for him or her; I stopped thinking that maybe I could provide that. That night, on the way to our last Lamaze class, I told Andrew about my day.

"Hmmm, that must have been hard to read about the families," he said, looking at me with real sympathy. "But they do sound pretty great. So is that it? Did you pick that couple?"

"No," I replied. "I'll do it the next time I go up. I had to think about it a little more. But I think they're the ones."

He nodded, eyes to the road. "Then I guess that's that," he murmured.

"Well, not yet," I said. "Have you signed the papers?" I had to wait to sign until after the baby was born, but he could go sign whenever he wanted. I was a little surprised that he hadn't already done it, given his resolute attitude about the whole thing.

"No, but I will," he said. "I haven't been up that way lately."

"Well, my due date is only two weeks away," I said. "It's better to have as much done as possible ahead of time, and we want this all to go smoothly." I was just parroting Jane's words to him. I didn't know much, but I did know it wasn't all going to be smooth sailing. It just didn't work that way.

I didn't find out until many years later that Andrew had a very tough time the day he signed the papers. I never knew that he, like me, sat in the car at first; that he remembered, years later, exactly where he had parked, exactly how he felt signing the papers; that it was a very moving, sad memory. At the time, I knew it was all a sad situation for him, but I had no idea of how sad . . . that he kept putting off signing the papers until the last minute. I had no idea.

showtime

My due date, November 2, came and went. I was Lamaze prepped, had my coach on standby, and had everything ready with The Cradle. At that time, the average hospital stay for a normal birth was three days, and Jane had strongly suggested not making the final, FINAL decision until after the birth. I kind of felt like I'd thought about it for the past nine months and wasn't likely to change my mind, but I went along with her, saying I'd wait. I continued working, not wanting to sit at home thinking about everything. Nobody at work said much anymore . . . it had been dissected and discussed ad nauseam, and everyone just felt bad. They knew it wasn't going to help to keep going back and forth, so we just avoided the subject. There were no showers, no parties, no celebration. I was hugely pregnant with a ghost who was going to disappear very soon.

The plan was for my parents to drive up from Ohio to be with me when the time came. When my due date passed, they decided to make the trip so they could be there to take me to the hospital. They were so encouraging. Even at the eleventh hour, they continued to say they would support whatever decision I made, although I knew their personal opinion was that adoption was best. I was so happy when they arrived—it was like my team had landed. It was great to have them with me but so sad for the reason. Instead of the usual excitement and anticipation that grandparents have, there was a subdued atmosphere around my apartment and not much talk about the baby. They weren't terribly enthused to see much of Andrew, either. While it wasn't anyone's fault, they knew how horrible this was for me, and they connected him with my pain.

After they'd been with me for a couple days, they took me to my doctor appointment, where I was pronounced primed and ready to go at any moment. The baby had dropped into place, and my cervix was busy doing its job dilating and effacing. On the way home, we talked about *the plan*.

"We will take you to the hospital," my mom assured me, "and we will stay the whole time. But Dad and I have been talking about it, and we think it will be too hard for us to see the baby. We both just adore little babies, and we know we will fall in love, and we don't think that's a good idea."

I got that. Certainly Andrew felt the same way. It was funny, though; I had the exact opposite inclination. Although I'd told Dr. Morgan that we would see how I felt at the birth, I knew I wanted to see and hold this little person who had become quite at home inside me, stretching and pushing my insides at whim. I knew I had to just get through this, but I had a curiosity and a love that needed at least some requital. In the face of my resolution that I was doing the right thing, deep down, I knew I would need that precious little time with my newborn. And then, suddenly, it was time. Pains in the night, a dash to the hospital, labor, labor, labor, and just like that, this unexpected, unanticipated, irregular, and incredibly challenging pregnancy was over, and Aimee Elizabeth was lying on my stomach.

your tiny nose

"A girl. I have a girl," I murmured. The small group around me stayed still and very quiet. All focus was on the baby, and no one wanted to spoil this moment with a sound. Looking back, I know it was not the normal process. The people in the room knew the circumstances, had no idea what to do or say, and so just stood there, watching.

"Aimee, you are so perfect," I crooned to her. I shifted her up so I could look at her; her lovely face, her miniature fingers and toes. She began to mew, and I gathered her up, holding her close. "You're here, precious girl; you're safe. I love you so much."

The hush in the room was deafening. Another minute or two passed while I whispered to her quietly, kissing her, and watching her teeny fingers grip my pinkie.

Dr. Morgan leaned over, not wanting to interrupt, but he did have a job to do. "Lorri, you're not quite finished here, and neither am I," he gently informed me. "You're about to deliver the placenta, and I have a small repair to do. Why don't you give Aimee to the nurse so she can clean her up?"

He saw the panic in my eyes and immediately reassured me. "Don't worry, she'll give her right back to you." I leaned back, putting myself back in his competent hands. My mind was completely full of Aimee. I didn't think about the future or my decision or Andrew or anything. I ached for her to be back in my arms and looked anxiously over my shoulder at the nurse who was administering to her.

Mariellen leaned over, squeezing my hand. "You did really well," she said softly. "And she is truly one of the prettiest babies I've ever seen."

Tears came to my eyes, and I agreed, "She is, isn't she? I'm not just a little biased?"

"No, no . . . she really is, and I just want to tell you how proud I am of you . . . and how much I admire you for what you're doing," she finished quickly.

I winced as Dr. Morgan finished his restoration on what used to be my private parts. They certainly weren't private right now. The nurse appeared with my darling baby girl all clean, measured, and swaddled, and I was completely distracted once again. People blended together down by my feet, cleaning and washing me off, while I couldn't take my eyes off the sweet child in my arms.

I turned to Mariellen. "I have a favor to ask. Could you please go tell my parents that they have a granddaughter? And could you tell them that they absolutely MUST come see her. They can't go away without seeing their grandchild."

Mariellen looked at me solemnly and promised she would convince them. As she walked away, I thought briefly about this veritable stranger who had taken on this kindness of tending to me and who had played such an intimate and important role on this rollercoaster day. Then I turned my attention back to Aimee, hoping that my parents would be able to understand that they simply had to see her. I knew they were so afraid to get emotionally attached, but she was such a miracle: so perfect! I was wheeled into the recovery room, and just as I settled into a deep discussion with Aimee, I looked up to see my parents walk in. Mariellen gave me a wink and walked out.

"You have to see her," I whispered tearfully. "You just CAN'T not see her." They stayed standing at the foot of the gurney, as though they dared not get too close. They peered over the tightly wound blanket to her porcelain doll's face and tiny pink pursed lips.

"Oh, Lorri, she is just precious," Mom cooed. "Such a gorgeous baby."

My father, who was a real pushover for tiny little girls (having had three daughters of his own), stood quietly, obviously smitten but concerned for me. "She's beautiful . . . now how about you? Are you okay?"

He was asking a normal question, but I knew what he was really asking. Should I be holding her, mothering her, loving her the way I obviously was?

"I'm fine, Dad," I replied, and I felt like I was telling the truth. Now that Aimee was here and I was filled with maternal love for her, I wanted the best for her more than ever. My resolve was strong. She deserved the best life possible, and nothing was too good for her. It was still clear to me that the couple I had chosen was hands down in a better position than I was to raise and care for her 24/7. But I had three days with her, and I was going to make the most of that time. I was going to hold her, talk to her, and give her a lifetime's worth of love before turning her over to her new parents. I looked at my dad and said, "Do you want to hold her?"

Both my parents shook their heads, and their sadness filled the room. "We can't do that," my dad mumbled. "We'll be outside if you need us."

I would find out later that they made several visits to the nursery over the next couple days to see Aimee, but they never held her. I, on the other hand, couldn't get enough of her. At that time, babies were kept in the nursery and brought in to the mothers periodically. Breastfeeding was just starting to make a comeback, but for obvious reasons, my breasts were bound to try to prevent my milk from coming in. I tried to keep Aimee in my room as much as pos-

sible. I took photographs, knowing well that these would be the only pictures of her I would have for a long time, if not forever. I would lay on my bed for hours, knees bent, with her on my legs, staring into her perfect face and talking to her about the life she would have. I would watch her sleep, marveling at her tiny nose

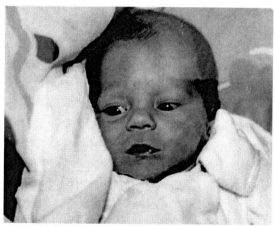

Aimee Elizabeth a.k.a. Katherine Anne, November 8, 1981

and lovely eyelashes. And I would tell her I loved her.

Flowers began to arrive, from family, friends, the *Donahue* office, and Andrew. I opened the card from Andrew and found a picture of a bedpan with a joke-y get-well wish. *Seriously?* Even now, with the grim reality of being on the brink of relinquishing our child, he wasn't going to break through that wall of protection and show some honest-to-God emotion.

"So how are you feeling?" he asked during a phone call the afternoon before I was to leave the hospital.

"I'm doing okay but getting nervous," I replied, staring into Aimee's eyes as she lay on my lap. Andrew hadn't been to the hospital to visit, because he didn't want to chance seeing Aimee, and we'd only spoken once since she was born. We were in uncharted, uncomfortable territory: like standing in the middle of a wobbly bridge between two points.

"Are you sure you don't want to see her, Andrew? She's so pretty . . . she kind of looks like you," I added. "You don't want to regret this."

"Yes, I'm sure," he replied nervously, and there was an awkward silence. "This is the only way I can do this," he said after a minute. "It's hard enough without having a face to picture."

As I hung up the phone, I whispered to Aimee, "I can't imagine not having this face to picture."

I spent the next hour trying to find a way to let the nurses take her away for the last time. I kissed her, held her, whispered to her, and stroked her tiny head. It was a desperate, gut-wrenching, soul-crushing goodbye, and then Aimee was taken back to the nursery. My sobs had just started to subside and I had just started to pull my heartbroken self together when the phone in my room rang. I was surprised to hear the voice of my boss, Phil, on the other end of the phone. I thanked him for the beautiful flowers he'd sent, and he asked how I was doing.

"I'm doing okay," I answered slowly, "but I'm dreading tomorrow."

"Well, that's what I'm calling about, and Marlo's here, too," he said. I sat up in bed—Marlo was there, too? What was this all about?

"Lorri, we know it's late, figuratively and literally, but we just had to put our two cents in before it really is too late," he began. "We'd like you to think about reconsidering your decision." He went on to insist that we could make it work; that I could bring Aimee into the office every day, that we could keep a crib there and figure it out, day by day. I was shocked into silence. His generosity and kindness were overwhelming, made even more so by my fragile emotional state. And then he put his wife on the phone.

"Lorri, Phil and I have been talking about this so much," she spoke in that familiar, husky voice I knew. I'd only met her a few times, and we hadn't really had any deep conversations, yet here she was, caring about what happened to my Aimee. These two bigger-than-life superstars had been talking about me and my situation, and now they were imploring me to change my mind. I couldn't think of a word to say.

"We just don't want you to make a mistake," she said gently. "You know, life throws you curves, and you never know what's going to happen. You could end up regretting this, and it will be final. You'll have no recourse."

I knew that. I knew it was final, but I also wanted the best life for Aimee, even if it meant that I lost her.

"You know, people take things for granted," That Girl continued, warning me. "What if you end up not being able to have more children? It's possible, and what if Aimee is the only child you could have, and she's gone? You just don't know what the future holds."

I stared out the window at the other end of the room, listening to Marlo make one good point after another, including things I hadn't really considered. I had begun to feel the old indecision inside me dusting itself off and finding its place on my shoulders when she handed the phone back to Phil.

"Lorri . . . look, we really don't want to interfere," he sighed. "I know you've given this so much thought. I've held off all this time with my opinion, but I just wanted to make sure you knew I would do everything I could to help, that we both care about you and Aimee, and we just thought we'd give it one last shot."

I felt the tears welling up. What wonderful people.

"I really appreciate your calling," I choked out. "I don't know what I'm going to do, but I love you for this, Phil, I really do. Both of you. Thanks for caring."

"I love you too, kid," he replied. "Good luck with this. We're thinking about you."

I sat there for an eternity staring into space—just thinking, just turning things over and over in my mind, and then quietly, subtly, a feeling of panic started to creep in around the edges. The black-and-white decision to choose adoption started to turn gray—*What if? Is this the right thing? Really? What if they're right?*

Sometime during the night, I fell asleep, and when morning came, I woke up racked with anxiety and indecision. My resolve was definitely caving, and it was almost time for me to leave the hospital.

Oh, Aimee, I thought frantically, the tears starting up again. *Three days have passed. I've held you and been with you as much as possible, and the whole time, I've known what I needed to do.*

But now I needed to do it. I needed to pass the nursery, knowing she was in there, knowing that I was leaving her there.

descending to hell

My parents arrived to take me home from the hospital. My face immediately told them that something was wrong. I started crying again.

"I . . . I just . . . I don't know," I sobbed. "I'm not sure . . . I don't know if this is the right thing . . . I don't know if I can do this . . ." My voice trailed off as the tears engulfed me.

"Call The Cradle," Mom said immediately. "They will help you."

I spoke to Jane, who quickly and calmly promised that I still had time to change my mind.

"Don't panic," she reassured me. "And don't rush this. Just don't sign right now. Go home, rest, and think about it. We'll take good care of Aimee, and you'll have a week to sign the papers if that's what you still want."

I continued crying as the two forces of reason battled inside me.

"But I don't want to wait . . . I want her to be with her adoptive parents as soon as possible. I want her to begin bonding with them right away. I don't want her all alone without a mother," I wailed.

Jane was steadily trying to comfort me. She told me again what the process was. Aimee would be picked up today and brought to The Cradle nursery, where she would be cared for expertly with love and affection by the nursing staff and volunteers.

"She will know she is loved, Lorri," she guaranteed me. "You don't have to worry about that. You have to take care of yourself right now and figure out what's best. It's very common to get indecisive at this point."

Indecisive. That was an understatement. I knew in the deepest part of my being that Aimee deserved the life I had prepared for her with the loving couple I had chosen for her. But I just couldn't bring myself to sign the papers. As the aide walked in with a wheelchair, I thanked Jane, told her I would need a day or two, and hung up the phone. I was shaking. The aide announced brightly that she was there to wheel me to the car.

"Honey, are you okay? Are you alright to do this?" My dad looked ready to take on anybody or anything that dared to move.

I looked from my mom to my dad to the suddenly nervous aide, who seemed to be trying to figure a way out of the room. It was obvious that this tension-filled room was not the scene of new motherhood bliss.

"Okay, okay . . . I can do this," I said, more to myself than anyone else. I gathered my suitcase while my parents put all the flowers and other bags and packages on the cart they'd brought in.

"I can walk," I said sullenly to the aide.

"Oh, no, hospital rules," she chirped, while taking my arm and helping me into the chair.

I started crying again as soon as we turned into the hallway. I will never forget the agony I felt as we rolled past the nursery. Was there not another way to get downstairs? Would it matter? My baby was in there! My angel . . . wondering when she would see me again. How heartless was I? How could I get in that car without her? I felt like I was hyperventilating, like I had been punched in the stomach and couldn't breathe. By the time we got to the car, I worried that at any minute, I would start wailing like an Irish woman keening at a funeral.

The poor aide, obviously not schooled on my case, gave my arm a sympathetic pat and sped away. I didn't blame her. If I could have escaped my life at that point, I absolutely would have.

My parents tried to take their cues from me on that horrific drive home. They were quiet while I wept and talked in hushed tones in the front seat when I was silent. There is no manual for what to do when your grown child is falling apart before your very eyes. They helped me up to my apartment, put me in my bed, and gently advised me to try to sleep. And then my hell began.

I had been violently ill for three days and was now jeopardizing my recovery. My incision area had blown up like a balloon from being constantly sick to my stomach. My breasts still throbbed a little from being bound, a reminder that I had no baby to nurse. I was completely undone, an emotional wreck. I felt weak and cried all the time. I was in a terrifying fog of fear: fear of making the wrong choice.

"What is the right thing to do? Dear God, please tell me; give me a sign," I would pray. "Every second that passes keeps Aimee from bonding with whoever will be her mother." I agonized over this point. It didn't matter who tried to reassure me that Aimee was fine and being loved. I hated that I was the reason she was still at The Cradle. I talked to Jane every day, telling her my dilemma, over and over. Each time, she patiently and peacefully listened and comforted me, and I would hang up with a promise to have a decision soon.

I had horrific nightmares of Aimee crying alone in the night and equally horrible daydreams picturing the adoptive family, waiting, wondering why they hadn't gotten the baby they were promised. I tried to put those thoughts out of my head, knowing that if I could just decide one way or the other, this agony would be over. My friends and family began to call, concerned that they hadn't heard from me and wanting to help. I would go over the pros and cons with each of them, back and forth, over and over, as if I'd never given it a thought until now.

I have to say I don't remember seeing or talking to Andrew during this most terrible week of my life. Maybe I did, but if so, it is totally blocked. This had to be a tough week for him too, but I only remember feeling absolutely, 100 percent alone, except for my parents, who wanted no part of making this decision. The phone would ring, and my parents would peek their heads in and ask if I wanted to talk to so-and-so. My doctor called each day, asking about my condition, and I figured my mom was probably calling him, worried out of her mind. When my condition went from bad to worse, Mom insisted on taking me to see Dr. Morgan.

After a quick examination, we met in his office. "Lorri, you should be healed by now," he said, sitting in a chair next to me. "And instead, you're in danger of opening everything up again. It's time for you to end this before you do real damage to yourself. You have to find a way to calm down, make a decision, and move on. This is wreaking havoc on your body."

I looked at my fingernails. "I don't know how to do that," I mumbled. "I sincerely don't know what I should do anymore." He looked at me sympathetically and put a hand on my shoulder.

"I don't have the answer for that," he said. "But the answer's out there. You have to find it and then live it. Embrace it. So you can have peace . . . and so can Aimee."

Back home, I sat on the couch and looked at my pros and cons list for the hundredth time. Dr. Morgan was right. I had to get ahold of myself and figure this out. I was doing nobody any good by drowning in this self-induced sea of distress. I thought about my conversation with Phil and Marlo. Up until then, I had been positive that I needed to give Aimee every chance at a happy life with a happy family. I considered Phil's offer carefully. Aimee in a port-a-crib, Aimee needing a bottle, Aimee the toddler careening around the office. Was this realistic? I could hope, but would it really work? I could see my colleagues getting frustrated listening to a baby cry or at a two-year-old pulling papers off their desks. I could picture myself anxiously comforting her, knowing I had five minutes to prep my guest for the next show. I didn't see how it could actually work without a full-time helper. I couldn't afford that, and this just wasn't Phil's responsibility to pay for another salary. It was a dream; it wasn't a true-to-life scenario. So now, I was right back to where I started with the same considerations and the same conclusions.

That afternoon, I got a phone call from my college roommate, Marianne, who had been staying in touch with me throughout the pregnancy. She listened to me describe the last week, inserting the occasional sigh of empathy and commiseration. She had a son a little over a year old, and I was sure she was wondering how I could be considering giving up my child. And then she surprised me. After a moment's silence, she started talking.

"Lorri, I just can't imagine doing this alone," she murmured. "And I've often thought, *How would I do this with a job?* It's really much harder than I ever expected, and although Stan is working a lot of the time, at least I do have him to help me when he's home. And your job is so much more than full time . . . I'm just not sure how you would manage."

I was not expecting to hear this. She was not judging me for considering adoption; she was endorsing it! Her words were an answered prayer. I realized that I had been judging myself. I felt guilty that I couldn't figure out a way to keep Aimee and feel good about the choice. Deep in my heart, I knew she would have a happier life with full-time parents rather than a piecemeal existence with an absentee mom. Marianne and I talked for about an hour, and she fully supported all the pros on my list for adoption. She validated all my reasons for choosing adoption.

I was still sad, and I was still grieving, but I felt a peace come over me that had been missing for a long time. Marianne had unknowingly given me the courage to sign the papers and let Aimee go to her adoptive family.

done

The next morning, November 13, 1981, five days after Aimee burst into the world, my parents drove me to Evanston and parked outside The Cradle's front entrance. Before I could get out of the car, they both turned around to face me in the backseat.

"We want you to know we are ready to stand by any decision you end up making today," my mother said earnestly. "We will wait patiently—you take all the time you need. We agree adoption is the right answer, but we know anything could still happen. We just want you to know we are here for you no matter what." I leaned forward and gave them both a kiss then walked up to the front door.

I knew somewhere in that building, Aimee was in a crib, waiting for me to decide so she could have a mother. I felt a pang in my heart and suddenly had a desire to run wildly through the halls until I found her, but I pushed the feeling down and walked through the door.

I sat down across from Jane, who smiled and asked how I was doing. She knew this wasn't my best day, and she listened intently to what I had to say. I was ready to sign the papers, but I had a few concerns. I wanted to make sure that I would be able to correspond with the adoptive parents and/or get information about Aimee from the agency. Although almost all adoptions at this time were closed, I felt as long as I could write every now and then or get an update once in a while, maybe some pictures, I could manage to do this. I had brought along some stationary, and I wanted to write a letter to the parents and one for Aimee.

"Well, here's how it works," Jane explained. "You can write those letters, and we will give them to the adoptive parents when they come for Aimee. But it's up to the adoptive parents whether or not they will respond or agree to communicate with you. My experience is that they will, but I can't make any promises."

I thought about that. What if they just disappeared? What if they wanted to keep Aimee as far away from me as possible? I thought about the people whose description I'd read and why I'd chosen them. I just knew those people would not deny me the knowledge that my child was thriving. I felt like I already knew them, and I decided to trust my instincts.

"Okay," I agreed. "I'd like to write the letters." Jane nodded and left me sitting in her office. I wrote first a letter to Aimee and then a letter to her adoptive parents, and I poured out my heart. Then I signed the papers and relinquished my baby girl.

Dearest baby,

I am writing this letter to you because I think it's so important for you to know what a special person you are. I want you to know how much you are loved.

The hardest thing I've ever done is to make the decision to let other people become your parents. Never think I did this because I don't love you. You are someone so precious to me, that I want more than I can tell you, and because you mean so much to me, I want you to have the best possible life. After a long time of thinking, both before and after you were born, I decided to give you to your mom and dad—for two main reasons. First, because they seemed like the very best of people and the most deserving of someone as special as you. And second, because I thought they could give you everything you deserve.

Your birthfather and I care so much for you, but we're not sure how we feel about each other. I'm not a teenager, and I'm old enough to have taken care of you, but I could never be with you as much as you'll need or as much as I'd want to be. To me, raising a child is too important a thing to do part time, and I couldn't stand to miss sharing your growing-up years.

I have a choice—to keep you with me and give you a mother who's gone working all the time and a father who's not able to be there at all or to let you go with two people who can be with you and make you their family and who need and want you as much as I do. That's what you should have. And loving you as I do, that's the only choice I have. As sad as it is for me, I'm happy knowing what a wonderful family you'll be.

I wrote poems to you while you were inside me, and I loved and cared for you all the time you were there. I watched and felt you grow, and when I watched you come into the world, I felt so proud—you are perfect. Everyone who sees you thinks you're the prettiest baby to come along in quite some time. There has never been a time when you were unwanted or unloved. In fact, everyone wants you, and because I love you so much, I'm giving you the best life that I can.

I've given you a name, and it's not the name itself that is important but the meaning. I looked for a name that means what you are to me, and I chose one that means beloved gift of God, or consecrated to God. And when you were born, the name fit perfectly. You are so beautiful, such a gift, and the hardest thing I've ever had to do is to part with you now. Please understand, I truly believe that this will make you happy. Please love your parents with all your heart. Because they are so good, I am able to do this.

I love you, my sweetheart.

Your birthmother

And to her adoptive parents:

Dear parents,

I feel like I know you both so well—I think I'd like you very much. It was so important to me to look very carefully for just the right people to raise this very special baby, but I never thought I'd find two people who seem to fit my idea of the perfect parents. I know you both probably feel so blessed to be getting a child, but I want you to know that I feel as though you are doing a great favor for me as well.

I guess my situation is not the usual one—I'm sure you've been told something about me, but I hope hearing it from me will help you understand. First, because the baby's father and I were not contemplating marriage, I was trying to be "a good Catholic girl" and felt that using birth control would be condoning the times I wasn't. This clever deduction resulted in my pregnancy. Abortion is something I would never consider, so my situation became creating a life and deciding on what to offer this life. It's taken me most of these months to make this decision, and naturally, it's still very hard. In fact, the reason you didn't receive her the day after the 72 hours is because I had to rethink my alternatives. I love her dearly.

I believe, absolutely, in the importance of the first few years of life and the impact of stability, security, and nearness during that time. I reached the decision that I could offer my child a part-time mother a couple hours a night and weekends and no father (he's been very supportive and stuck by me throughout, but at this time, there's no security of a lasting relationship) or that I could give her two people wanting a baby more than anything and able to raise her the way she deserves. Finding you only confirmed this thought. And believing the way I do, the guilt I would feel leaving my daughter every day with no grandparents and family in this city would be unbearable.

Being twenty-five, I think this adoption decision was unusually hard. Under different circumstances, I would love to raise a family, and this makes it all the more painful. There is a thought, though, that I am keeping to help me cope with this decision. Because I believe life is a gift, it's with this spirit that I give my daughter. God does things for a reason, and I believe that because I can't offer the best myself, I can give part of me to people who deserve a gift and who can offer the best. This helps me look at this not as a tragedy but as a situation from which a lot of good will come. This has helped me with the decision, and I hope it will help me go on afterward.

I want you to know also that in making this choice, I have accepted absolutely that you are this baby's mother and father. I thoroughly believe that parents are the people who get up at night, change diapers, teach and guide and worry and raise. I would never want to threaten that relationship, because, as I said before, I feel you are helping me by being people to whom I can entrust this responsibility. Knowing this, I hope you will feel secure in letting my baby know my love for her and my motivation behind all this. I hope you will feel free to someday give her the letter I've enclosed for her, so she'll hear from me how I feel (also, please feel free to read it yourselves). I believe that it's so important for her to know that her adoption is a result of being loved, not unwanted.

In terms of the future, I've seen too many families damaged by a child's obsession with finding out "where her roots are," and I never would want this to happen to your family. I truly believe that you have no reason to feel a threat from me (as I hope this letter has made clear), and if she does choose to search me out when she's older, I hope you will let her and stand behind her. I would be thrilled to see her again, and although I feel it is her place to decide, I would welcome her with open arms. I would also love to meet the two of you someday. I really do owe you so much.

It's true that I don't really know you two, but from what I've learned, I think I've made the right choices. This baby is so precious to me, and the only way I can abide by this decision is by knowing that she is getting two parents who deserve such a special child.

I would love to hear from you at anytime, if you'd like, especially in the next few weeks or months, just to know how you feel. The Cradle said that was up to you but that it would be fine.

My love and trust go to you for accepting the challenge of raising this child, and my heart goes to my daughter.

God bless you all.

The ride home was emotional, but very different from my horror ride home from the hospital. I cried, but I felt strongly that I had done the right thing. When I arrived home, a letter from my sister, Linda, was waiting for me:

Dear Lorri,

Right now, you are probably making the hardest decision you will ever have to make in your life . . . by the time you read this, you will have made that decision.

There is no way for you, Andrew, Mom, Dad, Kim, the Donahue staff, or me to know if your decision was the right or best one—yet we have all prayed about it. You have talked it over for nine months with people whom you respect and finally have reached an answer you felt was the best for both you and the baby. I truly believe that you must trust the Lord and know that your decision IS the best one or you wouldn't have made it.

Throughout this whole process, you have done everything so perfectly— thinking and planning so clearly and carefully. Saying I admire and respect you for the way you've handled this would be putting it mildly. I couldn't think of another person who could have handled the situation any better. You've been so strong, and now, through your decision, you will be released from this struggle and the burden in your heart, and the Lord will continue to bless you.

I love you so much, Lorri, and I trust your decision is the best possible one you could have made. Be content . . . you know we are all behind you always . . . no matter what.

All my love,

Linda

I put the letter back in the envelope and said a quick, silent prayer. I had gotten my sign. There was no turning back.

next . . .

I had arranged with *Donahue* to take a month off work after having the baby, go back home to Ohio, and try to regain my equilibrium. While packing to go, my parents informed me that they had arranged a trip for us. They felt that I needed to get away and totally relax and that November in Mexico was better than in Ohio. We would spend the first part of the month in Puerto Vallarta and the rest of the time in Ohio, including Thanksgiving, with the rest of the family. I was filled with love for them. Although me in a bathing suit was the last thing I thought the world would want to see, the fact that they were going above and beyond the call of parental duty to try to help me through this brought a surge of hormonal affection in their direction.

Before we left, I saw Andrew for a couple of awkward hours, where we talked around the subject of both of our lives blowing up. After telling each other that we would try to start again once I was back, my parents and I took off for Dayton. I sat in the backseat, thinking about what I'd just gone through. It was strange, but once I signed the adoption papers, an emotional bubble of protection seemed to descend and surround me. All the agony and physical pain from the indecision subsided, and, strangely, my emotions were almost deadened. During the five-hour drive, I welcomed the small talk my parents made about our upcoming trip and the family waiting to see me. I was happy to talk about anything and everything not involving Aimee.

I had moments where the hole inside got the better of me and the tears would start to well up. I would think about Aimee in her adoptive mother's arms or her adoptive father kissing her tiny cheeks. I would feel sad, but the tears wouldn't come, maybe because I was also feeling glad that she had a family around her who felt like they'd won the jackpot. The two of them were making her feel like the only baby girl in the world—a baby who made all their dreams come true. That was what I wanted for her. And I would put it out of my mind. I wouldn't cry. It was the oddest thing—I had either made my peace or lost the ability to feel. Something was dead inside, and I didn't want to explore it.

We left on our trip, and I will always look back and think it was just what the doctor ordered. It was a complete departure from the agonies I'd left behind: a total escape. We walked the beach, bargained with vendors, enjoyed great meals, bought souvenirs, went parasailing, and just relaxed. The three of us had been through an emotional war, and, little by little, we recovered our sanity. At my parents' sixtieth wedding anniversary party a couple of years ago, I told them that I would never forget what they did for me with that trip.

And I walked . . . miles and miles, sometimes with my parents, sometimes by myself. Occasionally, the tiny children selling Chiclets would bring Aimee to the front of mind, but most of the time, I focused on trying to regain my health and lose some of the baby weight, which was a constant reminder of my ordeal. It was not fun to have a postpartum stomach with no baby to show for it, but at least I was in the right place. Being a tall blonde with a little extra weight actually made me pretty popular in Mexico, which was a bonus for my self-esteem.

Back in Ohio, my family worked overtime to keep me busy and distracted. I would play with my nieces and nephew, which was a mixed blessing. They would remind me of Aimee, but they were also an outlet for the maternal hormones still left in my system. Their hugs and kisses did more for me than almost anything else.

The timing was good as I got back to work. The workload was slowing down as Christmas approached, so I wasn't swamped, but there was just enough to do to keep me sidetracked from thinking about my baby out in the world somewhere. My protective shield stayed firmly in place, and while people tried to walk on eggshells around me at work, and there were a lot of sympathetic glances thrown my way, I tried my best to convince everyone that I was doing alright.

The holidays came and went, providing lots of opportunities to distract me from the potential depression looming in the shadows. Friends called and invited me to parties, and my family insisted I come home for Christmas. Andrew and I resumed our relationship, but slowly. On our first night back together, we went out for dinner, and he laid out his game plan.

"I think we just have to start from the beginning again," he insisted. "Let's date. Let's try to get to know each other under normal circumstances. We have time now to see if what we have together is what we want."

I considered what he proposed. I could see it made sense to him . . . after all, that's what he'd been saying all along. He never saw her at the hospital, and he didn't want to see any of the pictures that I'd immediately developed and kept next to my bed. He'd never wanted her to be a real person. She was something that happened, something that put our lives on hold for a few months but was over now. For me, however, she was very, very real. Our relationship had gone through something extraordinary, which was not going to just disappear, at least not in my book.

I pulled my wine glass toward me and played with the stem. "Andrew, I can't just forget or pretend Aimee didn't happen," I replied. "But I do think we should try to put the past behind us and move forward. It's not going to be easy, but I'm willing to try."

He picked up his glass and clinked it against mine. "That's all we both can do . . . just try."

Sometimes it worked, and sometimes it didn't. We began to pick up the pieces, but it wasn't smooth or easy. We could have the best time just laughing or sitting on the couch watching TV, and then, inexplicably, there would be a wall between us. We continued going to movie premieres and *Donahue* events, although, after what had happened, I'm pretty sure he was a little uncomfortable around my coworkers who knew our story. In my mind, I think he felt judged by them. He had eventually confided in two of his friends and in his brother and sister-in-law, and we saw those couples often. They knew what we'd gone through, and Andrew could let his guard down with them. He still hadn't told the rest of his family, who seemed to accept that I was suddenly making public appearances again.

I came home from work one day in January after a long day of taping more than the usual roster of segments for the *Today Show*. After kicking off my shoes, I started going through the mail. Suddenly, I sat straight up, staring at the return address on the letter on top: THE CRADLE.

What was this? Why were they writing? A million thought bubbles started popping up on top of my head . . . was something wrong? Was Aimee okay? I started tearing open the envelope when another thought occurred to me . . . was it possible?

Yes, it was—Jane had written to tell me that there was a response letter from the adoptive mother and father for me. Would I like to receive it?

Oh, dear God, is there anything I would want more? Had I not been clear that I would always have an open door to ANY communication from them, that they didn't even have to ask? It was a miracle, a little gift thrown my way to ease the ache that never went away.

I called immediately the next morning.

"Jane," I blurted, "Of course I want the letter! Why didn't you just forward it to me? I can hardly stand the wait."

Jane was patient, as always, but I could hear her smile through the phone. "We have to ask, Lorri," she replied, "but I'll get it out first thing this morning."

The two days' wait was interminable. I was the opposite of patient, at times excited beyond belief and then angry that Jane had stolen at least two days of my having the letter. And then it was there, just sitting in my mailbox. With trembling fingers, I ripped it open.

Dear mother of our child,

We have been meaning to write ever since we picked up our precious little girl and brought her home. Your letter was very much appreciated, and I've been meaning to respond ever since we read it—but you can imagine how hectic things have been for us.

We just want you to know how grateful we are that you made the decision to give your baby up for adoption. We can only imagine how difficult the decision was for you and how painful the separation has been, just as you can only imagine the incredible happiness this child has brought to us. She means more to us than anything in this world, and you can rest assured that she will get as much love as any two parents can give.

She seems to be adjusting very well to her new home. She's really a good baby—very easy to take care of and extremely easy to love. We will save the letter that you wrote her for a time when she's much older and when we feel she can understand and appreciate it.

I could write pages more to you about her, but somehow I don't think that would help you any. Just know that our daughter will always know that her birthmother is a beautiful person who made the greatest gift you can make—the gift of love.

May God bless you all the days of your life.

Sincerely,

Her new parents

Wonderful. My first impression of Aimee's new mother was that she was wonderful. I loved her neat and graceful handwriting. I examined the letter; every word was read and re-read countless times. I felt an instant bond with her. She sounded like everything I could ask for in a mother for Aimee. She sounded smart and kind . . . and so loving. They adored my little girl; they were doting on her and knew how precious she was. The letter was like a soothing salve for me, reassuring me that my daughter was doing well and that I had made the right decision. I could almost feel a microscopic piece of my heart heal.

But, still, I didn't cry. Years later, it was suggested to me that perhaps I was surrounded by protective angels: angels that allowed in only tiny bits of the reality of my loss, or small portions of grief at a time, so as not to permit me to drown in my sorrow. Or perhaps my detachment was a result of the prayers of my family and friends, asking God to help me regain my emotional stability. All I knew at the time was that I was wearing impenetrable armor, protecting me from truly grieving the loss or feeling the emptiness.

sucker punch

I called Andrew and asked him to come over. I felt an obligation to keep him informed on any news regarding Aimee, even if he didn't want to see the pictures or really dwell on the relinquishing of our daughter. When he arrived, I asked him to sit down.

"So, before I signed the surrender papers for Aimee, I wrote some letters," I began. His body language immediately changed—he hadn't been expecting a conversation on this topic.

"I wrote a letter to Aimee for when she's older," I continued carefully, "and one for the adoptive parents, to kind of explain how this all came to be, and I gave them to the people at The Cradle."

"Okay," Andrew said with some suspicion and maybe a little apprehension. "So what's up?"

"Well, I think you should read the letters," I suggested. "And . . . I just got a letter back from the adoptive parents."

I waited, watching him. The defensive look on his face melted away to one of interest and curiosity.

"Really? That's amazing! What did they say?" I breathed a silent sigh of relief and handed him all three letters. While he read, I busied myself in the kitchen, sneaking peeks to see his responses. I was so happy to see his honest reaction to the correspondence: not the façade he put up to hide his emotions but the real person. It was reassuring to know, deep down, he did really care and that he wondered about Aimee, too. Even if he mostly hid those feelings, he was one of the few people who actually knew what the last year had held for me.

"Well, that's good," he said abruptly, laying the papers on the glass coffee table. "Seems like a great family . . . I think she'll be happy there." He sounded clipped and tense.

I hesitated and then asked one more time. "Would you like to see the pictures, too?"

He gave me a look that shut me down. "I told you, Lorri, I can't do that." The wall was back.

As the months passed, things with Andrew became more and more strained. Even though he began to tell me he loved me, there was a distance between us. I loved him too, but I thought he was holding back. Our relationship seemed to be stuck at a status quo, and sometimes I felt that we'd been closer before the baby was born. It seemed to me that Andrew was more himself during the time before Aimee was born than he was once his self-proclaimed "new beginning" started.

But he wasn't the only problem. There was a part of me that was broken, too. I thought I was trying to make it work, but I didn't even realize that I might never forgive Andrew for his role in making Aimee's adoption a reality. I tried not to dwell on it, and I thought I was doing an admirable job of leaving the past behind me, but I'm not sure I actually accomplished that. The subconscious is a powerful thing, and I think both Andrew and I had a lot of issues lurking below the surface.

Eventually, I was able to get to the point where Aimee wasn't on my mind every second of every day. Work certainly took over most of my time, challenging me with long hours and exciting assignments. It was easy to lose myself day in and day out, scouring the news for show ideas, booking episodes, pre-interviewing guests, and troubleshooting concerns. Still, every now and then, often late at night, I would pull out my stash of photographs and go through them slowly, one at a time.

May sweeps was a particularly busy time. We worked tirelessly to try to put together the very best shows for the rating period. Finally, we were headed into the summer hiatus, a time for us to catch up on all the stuff that had piled up on the desks as well as our personal lives. It had been about five months since I'd received the adoptive mother's letter, so I decided to write to The Cradle to ask if there was any new information about Aimee. She never really left my mind, and, although I had tried my hardest to return to my pre-pregnancy life, I was anxious to just hear that all was well. I sent off my letter, asking if there happened to be any news, letters, or photographs.

About a week went by, and each night, I would check the mail, hoping for the best. One night after work, I opened the mailbox and there it was . . . a letter from The Cradle! My heart started to speed up, and I couldn't help but feel excited. In the elevator, I pinched and manipulated the envelope, but no, there were no pictures enclosed. I felt a squeeze of disappointment in my stomach. *That's okay,* I encouraged myself. *At least there's a letter!*

I threw my purse and workbag on the table and settled into a big chair to open the letter. I eagerly gobbled up every word on her development and progress. Jane explained that the information was from the final pediatrician's report and reflected Aimee's growth through her first seven months :

> *Sleeps through the night . . . no allergic reactions to food . . . 17.5 pounds . . . eyes are gray-brown . . . wavy brown hair . . . just started crawling . . .*

I was smiling and chuckling as I read descriptions of my darling girl's stats and personality.

> *Extremely curious . . . very responsive to people . . . favorite activities: books, pushing herself around in a walker, looking at herself in the mirror.*

Then Jane added a few sentences about Aimee's adoptive mother and father.

> *The parents continue to be overjoyed with her and are truly providing her with excellent care and an abundance of love. They have adjusted well to the responsibilities of parenting and have not encountered any problems.*

Yay! That was so reassuring. I breathed a sigh of relief and went on to the last paragraph.

Shock and horror coursed through my body as I skimmed through and then went back and carefully read each word.

> *Well, Lorri, as you know, we will not have any more formal visits with this family, so we cannot offer you further information on Aimee. I hope you trust that she is doing very well and is in a very secure and loving home. I hope all is going well for you.*

Wait, wait, wait. What was she saying? What did she mean "cannot offer further information"? This was not right; this was not what we agreed! All the emotion I'd spent months pushing away came bubbling to the surface. There had to be a mistake. I ran to my bedroom closet and yanked out a small bin. I grabbed the file where I kept all the paperwork that pertained to Aimee. I snatched the top letter, the one that Jane had enclosed in January with the adoptive mother's response to the letter I wrote the day I surrendered Aimee. My eyes frantically searched Jane's written words.

Enclosed is the letter . . . hope it reassures you . . . respect and gratitude for you.

Then the paragraph I was looking for:

Lorri, I will ask you to contact me if you want more information about how she is doing. I would say by June we will have the final report on her development and progress, and if you want this information, you should contact me.

Nothing about NO MORE CONTACT. Nothing about NO FURTHER INFORMATION. The pediatrician's report was final, but no one ever said it marked the end of my tenuous connection to Aimee.

I sat on my heels on the floor with the letter in my shaking hands. There had to be a mistake. *Calm down, Lorri.* I took a deep breath. *You will fix this tomorrow. It's just a mistake.*

After a sleepless night, I walked to work, trying to calm my frantic nerves. I shut the door to my office and waited for the clock to strike nine o'clock then quickly dialed the familiar number and asked for Jane.

As soon as I heard her voice, I started talking.

"Jane, I got your letter. What do you mean you can't offer further information? What does that mean? That's not what we said."

There was a silent pause while Jane tried to figure out what I was referencing.

"Well, let me look at the letter," Jane replied, always calm. I heard the shuffle of papers. "I was just saying that the six-month mark has passed, and therefore, your case is closed. According to Cradle policy, no more information or pictures may be exchanged."

I was quick to retort. "Jane, that was never explained to me. I was told that if the adoptive family agreed, which they have, we could exchange letters and pictures. I haven't wanted to bother them, but she needs to know this policy so she can give you the okay to deliver letters from me."

Jane broke through my torrent of words. She spoke with sympathy, but confusion. "Lorri, you knew the adoption was final at six months, right?"

"Of course!" I cried. "I haven't changed my mind about the adoption! But part of how I made peace with this was knowing that I would have updates, that I might see her face now and then in pictures. And I knew it was at the adoptive family's discretion, but I chose them in part because they seemed so open and caring. I knew they would agree to this, and they have!"

Jane was quiet and then said, "I'm so sorry, Lorri. I don't know how this happened. You must have misunderstood me about it being final at six months. I can't apologize enough."

My voice was low and intense but quavering. "I don't want your apology, Jane; I want your help. This cannot be the end game." Every persuasive skill I'd acquired at *Donahue*, every way I knew to not take no for an answer, came into play. "I know there must be a way to get a letter to them, to let them know what has to be done. Is there someone else we need to talk to, someone in charge of these policies? I don't understand why you, as their representative at The Cradle, can't get in touch with them."

Jane answered, "There are very strict policies about contact. And they were put in place to protect everyone: adoptees, adoptive parents, AND birthparents. Once the six-month mark has passed, we are just not allowed to interfere in the family's lives. We are to leave them alone to raise their child without The Cradle intruding."

"But what if there was a medical issue?" I interrupted. "Or something of great importance? What if it was life or death? What would you do then?"

Jane replied with compassion, "Lorri, I know this means a lot to you, but it's not life or death."

"Maybe not for you," I muttered. "I sure feel like someone died. Please, Jane, please look into this. Please see what you can find out. Maybe if you explain the circumstances, if you tell them it was never explained to me that *final adoption* meant *final contact*; that I thought we had our own arrangement. And that we know the adoptive family is fine with this."

As always, Jane took her time answering. "Lorri, I promise to do my very best. I will talk to those in charge, but this is a board decision. It would mean a change in policy, so I wouldn't hold out a lot of hope."

At that, my tears started. "Jane, please," I begged, crying. "There has to be a way."

Jane promised to be in touch, and we hung up. I was completely overcome. All the tears I never cried over the last seven months now poured freely and seemingly without end. The emotions I subconsciously buried the day I signed the surrender papers came teeming to the surface. This, now, was the devastation, the door closing. I felt like Aimee had just been ripped from my arms, and the agony was palpable and unending.

After about half an hour, I got up and walked into the office of my boss, Wendy. She took one look at my face and jumped up, coming around the desk.

"What?" she demanded. "What happened? Are you okay?"

I could hardly form words. "Wendy, I have to go home. I can't stay here right now. I'm so sorry. I'll be back tomorrow."

She pushed me into a chair and pulled another chair up to mine.

"Tell me, Lorri. What's happened?"

Wendy, never married and not a mother, would never understand. She had tried to remain impartial during my pregnancy, compassionate but never weighing in on the decision process. I was pretty sure she wondered the entire nine months why I hadn't had an abortion. She was a talented producer, stoic, no-nonsense, and tough. As I sat sobbing, I tried to think what to tell her. I had nothing. I decided to go with the truth and waited for her to tell me to pull myself together and get back to work.

When I'd finished telling her the story, she quietly said, "I'll call you a car," and without another word picked up the phone and placed the call. "Go get your stuff and take the car home," she ordered me. "Take as long as you need."

I almost lost it again. People were always surprising me.

the dam breaking

That night, Andrew came over, and I told him what happened. True to form, he seemed to have sympathy, but it was only for me. As far as he was concerned, nothing had really changed for him.

"Maybe it's for the best," he offered. "Maybe you'll move on faster, and your life can go on. This could be a good thing. Closure."

I stared at him, through tears, in amazement. He just didn't get it. There was a major abyss between us on the subject of Aimee. His intense insistence to put her behind us didn't jive with my equally intense desire to keep a part of her in my life. I knew she belonged to someone else, but that fact could not erase that she came from me and that I would always love her.

I started crying again. "Yeah, maybe. Except it's not a good thing. It's a terrible, shocking, horrible thing that has opened every wound inside me. I WAS getting on with it, I HAD closure, but I expected to have something, some concrete information now and then to help with that closure. I feel betrayed, and I'm angry, and I guess you don't understand that."

He looked at me, and I could see the closing of the curtain across his face. "No, I guess I don't," he said, and, once again, I felt the distance.

I waited on pins and needles for some word from Jane. It seemed like a month passed, but it was just a week or so when another Cradle envelope appeared in the mailbox. Jane said she'd spoken to her superiors who had met with their board. There would be no exceptions. It was a blanket policy, and they were sorry, but they could not change it. I just could not grasp this. And I wasn't going to take this sitting down. Fortunately, Jane went on to give me two tiny kernels of hope.

I encourage you to write to the board, she wrote. *Policy can change, and you should let them hear, in your own words, how you feel. You never know, and nationally, there are starting to be more cases of open adoption. Also, if this family should decide to try to adopt a second child, and if they should come to us for the adoption, that would open the records again. We would have a window to get a letter to them.*

There was a lot of *should* in that sentence, but it was something to hold onto. I could hope. And I could fight back. With tears streaming down my face, I started to draft a letter to the board, but it sounded too despairing. I decided to let a few days pass. After the effects of the emotional sucker punch subsided just a bit, I picked it up again, ready to do battle. I probably started and stopped a thousand times. I'd lay it aside for a week or two and then take it up again, feeling the stress. It had to be perfect. It had to plead my case without sounding too desperate; it had to be measured, thoughtful, and persuasive. I had to explain how devastatingly unfair it was to lump everyone's situation together under a blanket policy. I was hoping that the board would see that each set of circumstances was completely different and should be judged as a unique case. In our situation, both parties had agreed to communicate. How could red tape stop that from happening? Finally, a month later, I put a letter in the mail.

Dear Jane,

About a month ago, we spoke and discussed my feelings concerning contact (through pictures and updates) with my baby girl, Aimee. At that time, you mentioned The Cradle's policy of no contact after six months, regardless of the circumstances. You may recall my surprise, since I had understood your policy to allow information to be exchanged provided the adoptive parents consented to this. After hearing my argument, you suggested that I write, expressing my views on this issue. This is a difficult assignment, as it seems that the outcome of this letter, and the chance of my view being accepted, may depend on the wording that I choose. Therefore, I ask in the hope that somehow my intentions might be clear, that you will look past the possible inadequacy of my words to the importance of their meaning to me and many others.

What I am asking for is simply a picture, now and then, of my daughter, if the adoptive parents consent. At the time of my request, you informed me of

The Cradle's policy concerning this, suggesting that such a move might reestablish lost feelings and instigate a desire for further and perhaps more intrusive contact. My argument is as follows: each case is uniquely individual. Seeing a picture or hearing about Aimee will not make me want her more or move me to an irrational action. As a twenty-six-year-old adult, my decision to relinquish my child to an adoptive couple was not an impulsive one but rather a carefully considered and mature one. I did it for her welfare, not mine, and I would never do anything to hurt her. Nothing, however, will make me miss her more or make me think of her more often. I think of her every day. I am simply asking for something tangible, so I might feel better about her welfare, and I do not feel that this maternal curiosity is wrong or unusual.

I now understand your basic policies, and I'm sure, in many cases, these policies are wise. For myself, however, it would only serve to assuage the continual pain. One of the reasons I chose this particular couple to be Aimee's parents was their apparent open attitude in these matters. Had I known future contact was out of the question, I might have taken a very different route. As it is, the misunderstanding is most unfortunate; however, a slight amendment in policy could rectify this situation and make things more reasonable for everyone.

Therefore, I ask you and your board to consider each case and request on an individual basis, according to the needs and stability of each person. My request, to receive occasional pictures and updates on my daughter, might seem harmful coming from one birthmother and perfectly reasonable from another. It seems to me that there is no harm in informing adoptive parents of a request, and if consent is given and the board approves, information should be exchanged through The Cradle.

I feel, in my case, my decision to give up Aimee was done for her good, so that she might have a full, well-balanced life. I do not feel that I should be punished for this for the rest of my life, and I do indeed consider the present policy a punishment . . . I ask only to be treated as a unique case, as I feel each case should be treated. A blanket policy may work in business, but not in these matters. I trust that you will do all you can, and I ask that you respond quickly. I would be happy to speak with anyone concerning this if there are any questions.

Thank you.

Cordially,

Lorri Antosz

I had given it my best. Now I just had to wait. Meanwhile, between my stressed and depressed state and Andrew's warm/cold relationship tactics, I began to feel like we were going nowhere. We were no closer to figuring out who and what we were to each other. One minute, he would be lovey-dovey, romantic, and attentive, and the next, he would pull away and seem cold and unfeeling. It was as though we'd passed a point of committal and he couldn't quite bring himself to go back there. I was losing patience. Something inside me had snapped when the umbilical cord of communication was cut at The Cradle, and I wasn't willing to put up with the nonsense of this game of cat and mouse.

I finally decided to take his advice and get on with my life. I broke up with Andrew. Our relationship seemed like nothing but work, work that wasn't paying off in any way, shape, or form. We both seemed miserable, and yet we seemed addicted to staying together. There wasn't a big fight or a huge cross-roads: one night, we just got tired of trying so hard, and I left.

Following our breakup, I tried to actually do what I'd set out to do—move forward. It was summertime, so work wasn't busy, but I dove into organizing and planning for the fall. I started renewing old friendships and going out now and then. And then the universe threw me a bone. One late afternoon, after everyone had left and I was reading through files, the phone rang.

"Hi, I'm looking for Lorri Antosz," said the voice on the other end of the phone.

"That's me," I replied, not looking up from my papers.

"My name is Marc," said the voice, "Marc DeAngelo. I went to school with your sister, Linda, in Arizona, but I live here outside Chicago. She told me to look you up, so I thought I'd give you a call."

I laid the papers down and thought for a minute. *Interesting.* I wasn't looking to get into another relationship so soon; that was for sure. But it would be fun to meet someone new, go out, and just have fun. It could be a great way to take my mind off Andrew and Aimee and all the pain of the last year. I agreed to have dinner with Marc the next night.

The next day flew by, and before I knew it, the guard was calling me to tell me my ride was downstairs. I gathered up my bags and headed to the elevator, wondering what I'd gotten myself into. I had just been through the mother of all relationship dramas, and what I needed was some downtime, not to dive into something else. I walked out the door, and there was a huge gray pickup truck with a very tall, very muscular, VERY handsome young man leaning against it. Someone upstairs was looking out for me. It turns out that the one thing I needed at that time in my life was an adorable Italian distraction.

For the next few months, Marc kept my mind off everything. We played golf every weekend, we went out with his friends and my friends, and we spent time with his family. In spite of my pledge to remain unattached, he quickly became my plus one, and we began going everywhere and doing everything together. He lived in the suburbs, and we did suburban things: barbecuing, going to the movies, talking into the night, and not worrying about anything. It was the exact opposite of my life with Andrew. I didn't have to wonder where our relationship was going . . . it was going just fine. I didn't have an enormous emotional roadblock named Aimee standing in between us. We just had fun. I told him about my daughter after a few weeks. He listened with interest, felt bad for me, and immediately tried to take my mind off the subject. Marc was just what the doctor ordered. Not only was life easy and simple, but we were always active and busy, and what remained of any baby weight dropped off, and then some. I began to feel my old self returning; I was no longer weighed down figuratively or literally.

Every Sunday, we had dinner with his family. This was non-negotiable, and I didn't mind a bit. His very Italian mother cooked a full-blown feast, and Marc and his sisters were expected to be there. We would eat like kings and queens, and, although it was a treat to have amazing home-cooked meals, it was also a preview of what life would be like were I to seriously become involved with Marc. He and his father were the kings, and the ladies of the household were definitely there to take care of them. Having worked for Phil for a couple years, my feminist leanings were not amused. Still, he was what I needed at that point in my life.

One evening, I was working late when the phone rang.

"It's Andrew," a familiar voice said.

"Oh . . . um, hi," I stalled, not even having the presence of mind to ask a single question. I was not expecting this call.

"How have you been?" he asked brightly.

"I, uh, I've been good," I stammered. "Busy . . . the fall season is starting soon . . . busy."

"I've been thinking about you a lot," he went on. "I mean, a lot. I'd really like to take you to dinner and talk. I think we have a lot to talk about, actually."

I didn't answer. "I'm not sure, Andrew," I finally said. "I . . . well, I think it's been good for me to not talk about everything."

"Yeah, well, that makes sense," he said, still sounding more upbeat than I'd heard him in a long time. "So, maybe we just start out simple, just see each other."

I took a deep breath. "Andrew, I've kind of been seeing someone," I admitted. I didn't mention that it was light and easy and uncomplicated, and I didn't say that I'd started to wonder if it was time to let Marc find a nice, old-fashioned Italian girl. I was afraid to say much of anything.

Andrew seemed to mull that over a bit. "Yeah?" he questioned. "And you can't see anyone else?" I was impressed with his careful, non-jealous answer.

"I'm not sure I'm comfortable with that," I finally got out.

"Well, is it okay for us to just talk now and then?" he asked. "Just to catch up, be friends? I miss you." He was saying all the right things, and we had so much history that it was hard to just shut it all down.

Over the next few weeks, it became a rope-pull contest of feelings. Andrew called every few days, just to say hi, and after we would talk, he would send flowers. I would get drawn in to our familiar, affectionate patterns. Then I'd go out with Marc, and he was like a boy who made me laugh. I'd go back and forth, feeling torn between staying safe where life was easy or taking a chance on something deeper but infinitely darker. I had grown so very fond of Marc, but I think subconsciously I knew we were never going to be a match made in heaven.

Meanwhile, work had gotten very busy again. Phil's affiliation with the *Today Show* came to an end, and he was offered yet another opportunity. ABC came to him with a chance to do *The Last Word*, following Ted Koppel on *Nightline*. It was a chance for Phil to do the kind of journalism he loved best: hard news and political guests. Our little production staff moved over to the ABC offices, and our team was enlarged with a couple of truly wonderful and entertaining producers. As much as I loved the work we'd done at NBC, I was thrilled with the new adventure, and I loved my new partners in crime.

I had another decision to make during this time, which was made even more difficult by the limbo in which I was stuck between Marc and Andrew. It turns out there was yet another layer to Phil's generous spirit. I had no idea that he had a tradition of celebrating every five years on the air with a fantastic staff trip. Earlier in the year, at a party at his house in Winnetka, I was shocked by a presentation telling us where we would be going to celebrate fifteen years on the air. We were led, step by step, through what would be an amazing tour of France, including a river barge trip, hot-air ballooning, and five-star accommodations in castles and Parisian luxury hotels. Everything and everyone was included, even a plus one.

It became increasingly awkward as the summer progressed and the travel manager needed to know who was going on the trip. I didn't feel like Marc and I were in the kind of relationship where I would feel comfortable whisking him off to Paris. And even though I was back on speaking terms with Andrew, we weren't even really dating. It wouldn't be fair to take one of my sisters over the other one, and I was still young enough that I thought it would seem juvenile to take my mom. It was coming down to the wire, and I needed to choose my trip partner.

One night, I was talking on the phone to one of my best friends, a sorority sister from Cincinnati. She had been one of my main confidantes while going through my pregnancy and had done housing research in Cincinnati for me when I had thought about moving back to Ohio. I knew she was one of those friends who would always be there for me.

"So, how would you like to go on an all-expenses-paid trip to France with me?" I asked spontaneously in the middle of our conversation. I wondered if that was quite possibly the most fantastic question anyone could ever ask.

"WHAT?" she sputtered. "What are you talking about?" She knew about the trip and about my quandary, but I don't think either one of us had ever considered this possibility.

"Why not?" I countered. "We would have a blast."

After checking with her husband and her work, Maureen was quick to call and accept the invitation. She told me she felt like she won the lottery. "You're not the only one," I assured her. "We all feel that way!"

A week later, Marc and I parted on friendly terms, each knowing our relationship had been fun, loving, and carefree but not the stuff of a lifetime together. We would never be what the other was looking for, but I will always be grateful Marc was there when I needed him.

The next time Andrew called, he asked again about going out to dinner—a real date.

"Hmm . . . really? Is this a good idea?" I was pretty sure it wasn't. I missed him, quite a bit, actually, but our history came with a lot of baggage. We'd only been apart about four or five months.

"I don't think it's a bad idea," he laughed, and I realized I missed that easy, contagious laugh. I hadn't heard much of it in the months before our breakup, and it sounded good.

"Let's just go to Gordon's and see how that goes." *Gordon's?* Gordon's was one of Chicago's finest restaurants. It was both suspicious and irresistible. I decided that one dinner wouldn't do anyone any harm. I still cared a lot for this man, and people did talk about second chances.

light switch

ndrew was on his best behavior: charming, funny, sweet. I remember thinking that maybe enough time had passed and maybe the separation had done us good. He sent me a beautiful arrangement of flowers the next day at work, and before I knew it, we started right back where we left off. He was romantic and full of declarations of love; I started to get pulled back in.

Of course, this made it a little awkward when it was time for the *Donahue* trip to France. It would have been fun to go with Andrew, but all the arrangements were made. Looking back, I'm glad I went with Maureen and just had an easy, uncomplicated vacation. Sometimes, it just takes a girlfriend!

Andrew and I didn't really talk much about Aimee during the fall of 1982. There wasn't a lot to say. I had not heard back from The Cradle board, although I had spoken from time to time with Jane. There were no policy changes yet, although she said they had been impressed with my letter and were at least discussing new options. In order to be sane, I had to just continue with my life, but it was a struggle. I'd done what I could, but maybe nothing would come of it. What if I never heard from Aimee or her family again? I had to put my hopes on a shelf and wait . . . perhaps write another letter to the board in a few months.

We spent Aimee's first birthday quietly at home, without a lot of discussion and certainly no celebration. It was, in some ways, a time of honest, sincere closeness; we quietly shared the loss of our child without really probing into what it meant to us. We still avoided the big questions. There was something that pulled us together, but neither one of us really knew what it was. Having to deal with such a monumental life issue before we even knew the other's favorite color seemed to short-circuit our relationship.

Years later, I would find out that in the months before Aimee was born, Andrew couldn't figure out if I loved him or was just throwing everything I had at him, especially all the glamour that came with my *Donahue* job, in an attempt to make him stay. In my eyes, he was just unwilling to give us a try, and as a result, we lost our daughter. After Aimee was gone, it seemed to me that Andrew couldn't seem to let me go but, at the same time, couldn't quite try hard enough to hang on, either.

For a few months, it seemed possible. We had a time of feeling close and hopeful, and I allowed myself to think that maybe, just maybe, this might somehow work out. But no . . . almost as soon as I began to relax and feel comfortable, Andrew started to retreat into some of his old habits: emotionally distancing me and drawing back into his shell. It was as though he knew he had me back, and not only was he taking me for granted, but it seemed like he was scared of the direction we were headed. I recognized the signs and decided to face it head on.

"Andrew, here we go again," I told him one night. "What is going on with you? You're pulling away from me again, and I don't understand why."

He didn't answer at first but then admitted, "You're right; I know it's weird right now. I think we're just not on the same timeline." He paused, glancing at me sideways. "I think you're ready for a commitment, and I'm not there yet. I know I love you, but I'm not sure when I will be who you want me to be."

I'd been in one four-year relationship and several shorter ones and had already invested two years with Andrew. I was almost twenty-seven years old. I decided that, for me, "I'm not there yet" translated to "goodbye." I wasn't willing to get into another long-term, go-nowhere relationship, no matter what history we shared.

This began a long makeup/breakup cycle with Andrew. For the next two years, we rode a strange roller coaster ride. I began dating other men, and soon after, he would begin a campaign to get me back. Phone calls, flowers, gifts of epic proportions would be showered upon me until I would finally give in, only to fall back into the same patterns once we'd established our relationship again. The strange thing was that he kept coming back and I kept allowing him back in my life. It was almost like the definition of insanity: repeating the same action over and over and expecting a different result.

We always had fun together. We had a similar sense of humor, similar goals, and similar backgrounds. And then there was the whole part of going through a major life struggle and coming out on the other side still caring about each other. On paper, it seemed like there was no reason this shouldn't work. Except, of course, there was one, and we just didn't know enough to realize that what we'd been through could produce comparable psychological reactions to what couples experience who have lost a child. Even though we had made this decision ourselves, the result was that we didn't have her, and this subconsciously haunted us both. I felt like I was trying, but every time Andrew and I would seem to gel and figure things out, he would pull away and sabotage us, and I was getting to the point of no return.

In the summer of 1983, we were broken up again. The ABC late night show, *The Last Word*, had ended, and our staff moved once again, this time over to CBS, where most of us were absorbed into the main show staff. I was promoted to producer and shared an office with the show's director. It was professionally so rewarding to now be responsible for entire shows, rather than short segments, and I loved being part of the main team. In addition, I decided to enter the real estate market, buying a two-bedroom townhouse that was scheduled to be built over the next nine months. As we entered the fall season, I felt secure and excited about my career and my independence, which was a good thing, because my love life was another story.

This time, Andrew had entered in the usual window: calls, flowers, saying all the right things. But having been around the block a few times with him, this time, I wasn't jumping through his hoops. I was reluctant to let him back in, even as all the familiar thoughts and feelings came storming back. It seemed, however, that he had a new plan.

"I'd really like you to come with me to see a psychologist," he informed me. "I think we need to sort through all the confusion and this back-and-forth, up-and-down thing that happens between us."

I wasn't sure at all that this was what I needed. I wanted more information on my daughter . . . that's all I needed. I felt ready to move on from Andrew; we'd been in an off cycle for a while now, and I was dating and doing okay. I explained that to Andrew, but he was persistent.

"Well, why not give it a try?" he asked. "Would you do it for me? I'm having trouble moving on, and I've started to see this doctor, and she thinks it would be good for us to do this together." Then he played the trump card. "She thinks Aimee has a lot to do with all our problems."

Well, this was a little tougher. I didn't really want to open another chapter of the same book; I already knew the ending. But maybe I did need to explore this strange addictive nature of our relationship and see if Aimee had something to do with it. Maybe if we could understand what pulled us together and pushed us apart, we could either finally be a couple OR finally go our separate ways. I agreed to go.

We sat on the couch together and looked at Alexandra. This was our eighth or ninth session with her. Since it was his idea, Andrew had insisted on paying the bills for our time with her. In some ways, I felt like I was along for the ride, and that ride was a Mercedes-Benz. It was such a luxury to pay someone to sit and listen to your problems and then to hear their objective opinions on your personal situation. If I'm honest, I'm not sure it changed anything or really helped us solve anything, but it did help us to understand our relationship, and it was interesting to do the exercises and try to connect the dots.

During the last session, Alexandra had delved into the fact that we had been apart on Aimee's second birthday. I had spent it alone at home, and it turned out that Andrew had spent it alone as well. We had both talked about how it was impossible to imagine that we had a two-year-old daughter growing up somewhere out in the world. I wondered what today's topic was going to be.

"So, Lorri," Alexandra looked at me. "Tell me why you think you always take Andrew back, given that he hasn't been able to commit to the relationship?"

I looked back at her, and then at Andrew, who had turned on the couch to look curiously at me too. "Well, I really don't know the answer to that," I said honestly. "But I haven't taken him back this time. I'm coming to these sessions with him, but we're not back together."

"Why is that?" she asked simply.

"I guess I'm afraid we'll just fall right back into the old patterns," I replied. "We've done this so many times, and it always ends up with him pulling away. It starts out great, and we're close and committed, and then he puts up all the walls and the intimacy goes away. It's like he can't make up his mind, and I just don't want to do it anymore."

"How much of this has to do with Aimee, do you think?" she probed.

"For me?" I asked. "I don't think it DOES have to do with Aimee. It has to do with Andrew and his inability to move forward."

Alexandra leaned forward, elbows on knees. "Do you know that studies of couples who lost children show that regardless of how their pregnancies ended, couples are more likely to split up if they are living together rather than married, if the mother is young, and if the relationship is less than one year old?"

I looked blankly at her. "Well, that's a trifecta for us," I said humorlessly, "and we weren't even living together."

"My point," she continued, "is that you're still here trying, and that is unusual."

"Trying . . . that's the optimal word here," I answered. "Not succeeding."

She looked at Andrew and then back at me. "Lorri, have you ever thought that maybe you just will never be able to forgive Andrew?"

"Forgive him?" I repeated. "Forgive him for what?" *Why is she so focused on me today?* I wondered. Wasn't Andrew the one who was having the big issues? Wasn't he the one who kept waffling and couldn't commit?

"Forgive him for refusing to figure out your relationship in time to save Aimee," she said matter-of-factly.

I stared at her. "Do you think that's true?" I asked.

"It doesn't matter what I think," came the typical psychologist's response. "What do you think?"

I sat there and thought about it. Did I blame Andrew? Did I secretly, deep down inside blame him for losing Aimee? Subconsciously, did I think if only he could have gotten his game together, we would be a family now . . . two parents and a toddler . . . Aimee would be ours?

I took my time answering and finally said, "I have no way of knowing that. Maybe. Maybe it's a secret I carry without even realizing it. But what does that have to do with why Andrew can't seem to move to the next level in our relationship?"

Alexandra sat back. "I think the root of all your issues is Aimee, both of you," she explained. "I think before your relationship had a chance to build a foundation, you were called on to make tough decisions. Most young relationships couldn't weather this kind of storm, but you two keep asking questions, keep trying to make sense of all this. Your relationship is addicting because you are searching for the reason WHY this all happened. There's something that is pulling you together and pushing you apart, and I believe that something is Aimee."

I was just trying to absorb the whole idea that Alexandra was putting out there. I knew Aimee was central to our problems, but I hadn't considered my part in this: maybe I was contributing to our hot-cold dynamics because I blamed Andrew. Suddenly, I began to soften once again toward him as the tears rolled down my face.

Alexandra continued her analysis. "Managing this kind of process is very difficult, and Andrew, I think when the two of you start to break down all the barriers and you feel very close to Lorri, you get very disturbed by the idea that you made a mistake, that you should have given yourselves a chance with Aimee. Except now it's too late, so to prove that you weren't wrong, you sabotage the relationship. It's all very deep rooted, in my opinion."

Andrew was sitting there nodding. I just didn't know, but it sounded plausible. I hadn't thought that it was Aimee for him at all, but maybe it was. It always seemed that he just couldn't allow himself to let go in the relationship. But maybe this whole thing with Aimee affected him as much as it affected me. It was possible.

We walked together back to my office. It had definitely been the most challenging session yet, and we were lost in our own thoughts. Then he grabbed my hand.

"I really want to start again with us," he said earnestly. "I want to make this work. I think if we know what causes our issues, we can do something about it."

I slowed down, shaking my head. "I don't know, Andrew," I whispered. "Knowing it doesn't fix it. And this is just Alexandra's theory . . . maybe she's wrong. We've been through so much. Maybe we should just cut our losses. I accept that it's possible that Aimee affected you way more than I ever knew, but the facts are that you have always avoided making her real. You set her in a box and put her away. You never saw her pictures, you never told your family about her, you never want to talk about her. How will knowing this change anything between us?"

We stopped outside the door to the station, and Andrew wrapped his arms around me in a bear hug. "I don't know, but I know I can't let you go." Something inside me melted a little bit, and I hugged him back.

CHAPTER EIGHTEEN

surprise, surprise

The next day, an enormous arrangement of gorgeous flowers arrived at my office. My coworkers gathered around, gawking and teasing me. I knew whom they were from, but I looked at the card anyway. The simple *I love you* spoke volumes. That night, he called and asked me to go to dinner the next night.

"I have a surprise for you," he said after I agreed to one dinner. He didn't mention he was bringing out the big guns to prove his dedication and show how he had changed. In his campaign to convince me to try again, he was calling in reinforcements. The next night was a very cold, windy evening. Andrew picked me up from work and told me we were meeting his parents at a lovely restaurant on Michigan Avenue.

"Your PARENTS?" I asked, completely shocked by the idea. "I didn't know they were in town."

"They weren't—they drove in this afternoon," he explained. "And there's more."

I was still trying to comprehend why his parents were joining us for dinner. It seemed awkward, especially since we weren't even really dating. I thought this was a dinner for us to sort out and explore some of the revelations from our session with Alexandra. "More?" I squeaked.

He pulled into a parking spot, turned, and looked at me sitting nervously in the passenger seat. "I told them," he declared. "I finally told them."

I was speechless. "T-t-told them?" I stuttered. "Told them what?"

"I told them about Aimee," he erupted. "I told them the whole story on the phone yesterday: about the pregnancy, and the adoption, and how messed up we've been. They jumped into the car this afternoon and came right down. They wanted to see you, too."

I sat there open-mouthed, taking the story in without much comprehension. I had no idea what I even felt—besides an enormous sense of being overwhelmed. *His parents?* I was just trying to figure out if I wanted to let Andrew back in my life, and now his mother and father were here. They were lovely, very sweet people, but I still had a lot to sort out between the two of us. It just wasn't the right timing for a come-to-Jesus family dinner.

The evening was exhausting emotionally as I tried to tap-dance my way through dinner, answering questions from his naturally curious parents and feeling all the old wounds opening up again. They were understandably wanting more details about how, when, why, and where we stood now. I'm sure all of a sudden, lots of strange, unexplained behaviors and absences were starting to make sense to them. I instinctively knew this and tried my best to give them the information they wanted about their grandchild while not committing too much about the future. I had to give Andrew credit—he had said he wanted to figure things out. Between therapy and finally telling his family the truth, he was convincing me that he did indeed want to make changes. Still, this was one surprise that threw me for a loop. I was caught unprepared and felt a little like a trapped animal. Fortunately, Andrew's parents were kind and sympathetic. When the four of us arrived at my apartment, everyone seemed to understand that I needed my own space to process the evening.

I stopped at the mailbox before heading to the elevator. I was emotionally drained and ready to just crash in bed. I pulled out the mail, and, stepping into the elevator, I began to sort through it. In the middle of the pack of junk mail and bills, I saw the now-familiar return address from The Cradle. My heart started racing . . . it had been fifteen long months since I'd received the letter from Jane telling me of the board's decision to stick with their policy: fifteen months with no news, no updates, no nothing. I didn't have a clue what this letter could hold, but I knew it couldn't be worse news than the status quo.

Once again, I dropped everything inside the door and ran to sit at the kitchen table. I ripped open the envelope.

Dear Lorri,

I am writing, as you requested, to let you know how Aimee is progressing. As I mentioned in the phone call, if her adoptive parents were to contact us for a second adoption, we would have current information on her. Well, they have recently requested consideration for a second adoption, and so I now can tell you that your daughter is doing very well.

She went on to describe Aimee's development on all fronts. Still with brown hair and dark eyes, Aimee was outgoing and friendly. She loved other children, had a great attention span, and was very bright. I drank in every detail and description, and then I dropped the letter and jumped in the air. *Yes! Yes!* It had happened! Finally, the door was open again. After the evening's events, I felt emotionally like I was going from zero to sixty without a car. The relief coursed through me in currents, and I could barely contain myself.

This meant I could get a message to Aimee's parents and ask them to put in writing that we could continue corresponding at will. This changed everything! The tears rolled down my face, and I suddenly knew what it felt like to want to shout something from the rooftops. This was the best news in the world, and it changed my entire frame of mind from the evening. I sat down to reread the letter, especially the update on Aimee. I had skimmed so quickly at first trying to figure out what the letter meant.

Amazing . . . Aimee was doing so well. It was crazy to think of her as a two-year-old toddler with dark brown eyes, walking at thirteen months, outgoing and friendly. I could just see her—and then my mind raced on to the next subject. To think that Aimee's adoptive parents had applied for another child . . . Aimee would not be an only child. That thought made me smile. Would she have a brother or a sister? Who cared . . . she would have a sibling; that's all that mattered. How great. I laid the letter back down, lost in thought. Their case was now opened, and there was a window of opportunity. I needed to make my case to Aimee's parents so they knew the urgency of having a letter on file that approved communication even if the records were closed. I just had to keep the conversation going . . . just in case.

Usually, any Cradle correspondence took me weeks or even months to carefully compose, making sure every thought was exactly right. I would labor over it, looking up grammar and triple-checking every sentence. Then I would type it up and go through the same checking process again. That night,

I grabbed a legal pad and wrote furiously. I was done in under an hour, and I didn't bother to wait until I got to the office to type it up. I walked down to the corner and put it in the mailbox that night. I wasn't going to take any chances that the window would somehow close before I had a chance to make my plea.

The next day, I called Andrew to tell him what happened. Still on a high from the previous night, he responded with a supportive "That's great!" but I could tell that this chance for me to get my foot back in the door wasn't as thrilling for him as it was for me. I'm sure a part of him was asking why I didn't leave well enough alone, but I was just happy that he didn't go down that road. I was excited enough for the both of us.

With the holidays approaching, Andrew and I fell back into a rhythm of being together and falling in love again. The evening with his parents combined with the last session with Alexandra had shaken my resolve to stay apart, and we began to date again. As was usual when we made up, things between us were warm, wonderful, and romantic. We attended all the seasonal events and parties, and it seemed like everything was right with the world. Phil always held a fabulous, glittering Christmas party at his lovely home north of Chicago, and we went, anticipating another fantastic night to get us in the Christmas spirit. We got a lot more than expected.

That night, Phil made an astonishing announcement.

"You all know that Marlo and I have been commuting between New York and Chicago for the entire five years we've been married," he began. "I made a promise to her that we would not do this indefinitely, that we would have an end date when I would move to New York. We finally have that end date."

The room burst into excited voices and muffled screams. This was big news for everyone there. Phil continued, "We will be moving the show to New York City, and our new offices and studio will be at NBC at 30 Rockefeller Center." We all gasped. *Working at 30 Rock? Only the most thrilling address in all of Manhattan!*

"You have plenty of time to decide what you want to do, but you are ALL invited to make this move and continue with me in New York. We will move over the break next Thanksgiving, and new shows will start from New York the first of January, 1985."

Everyone began applauding and yelling and laughing. It meant something different for each person there. For some, there was no question—moving to New York was a no-brainer, an exciting adventure that was not to be missed.

For others, with family and connections to Chicago, this meant their job would be over. They knew immediately they could not make such a drastic move. For most of us, it was complicated, and it meant we had a lot of thinking to do, but having the option to move to a city like New York was undeniably exhilarating.

I was in that last group, having just renewed my relationship with Andrew. I had no idea what this news meant for me, but I was pretty sure Andrew wasn't going to leave Chicago. On the other hand, this was a tremendous opportunity, and continuing to work for a generous, inclusive, dynamic man like Phil would be hard to turn down. We had a lot of talking to do.

In the car on the way home, I asked Andrew what he thought of Phil's announcement.

"It's crazy!" he answered. "Did you know he was going to move the show to New York?"

I laughed. "No! I had no idea!" I shook my head, still amazed by the night's news. "I guess I should have figured he wasn't going to commute forever, but I just didn't think about it."

He looked sideways at me. "What do you think you're going to do?"

"I . . . I guess I'm not sure," I said a little cautiously. "I think we should talk about it, that's for sure. I think it's a decision we should make together."

"Yeah," he agreed. "That's true . . . but I don't want to stand in the way of a great opportunity. I don't want to be the reason for you to have regrets." I looked at him ironically. Given our history, I kind of had to laugh at that.

We sailed through the holidays, and then 1984 jumped out of the gate. Between work starting up again, construction details with the townhouse, and all the excitement about the move to New York, the time seemed to fly. Multimedia, the company that owned *Donahue*, offered each employee an airline ticket and a hotel stay to go check out potential locations and housing possibilities. I flew with a couple other staffers to look at New York from a fresh perspective: as a possible new home. 30 Rockefeller Center was mind blowing. With the gorgeous Sistine Chapel ceilings, the ice-skating rink out front, the magnificent art deco details, and the state-of-the-art studios, it would definitely be an incredible place to work. The city seemed nice enough, although I loved Chicago and didn't really see why one would want to spend twice as much to live in the Big Apple. I looked at a few apartments just to get an idea and was horrified to see that my soon-to-be mortgage payment for my two-bedroom townhouse would not even cover a studio in NYC.

Maybe the idea that I would move to New York scared Andrew. Or maybe he'd had enough of our on-again/off-again shenanigans. In any case, when Valentine's Day rolled around, he invited me out for a special romantic dinner.

"Lorri, we've been to hell and back," he said to me as we shared a dessert after a mouth-watering dinner. I looked at him, wondering why he thought this was a good time to bring that up. "I know we've been anything but steady, but I know I love you, and I know I don't want you to move away."

He had my attention then, but I was still unprepared for his next question. "Will you marry me?"

Shocked, I tried to think of an answer, but this was a yes-or-no question. It was a question I'd wanted to hear from him so many times over the past few years, and yet now, I wasn't 100 percent positive of my response. There were so many variables now . . . most especially that the job I loved was moving to New York City. I knew I couldn't bring that up right at this moment, though, with Andrew waiting expectantly for me. He looked happy and excited. I couldn't let him down. And I did love him . . . so . . . "Yes," I whispered, and he slipped the exquisite diamond onto my finger.

The next few months were a blur of emotions. We discussed our options, examining the different scenarios of moving for my job or staying for Andrew's. It was clear that Andrew was not interested in the moving idea. He argued that my townhouse was nearing completion and it would be a shame to not get to live in it. He contended that I would easily find a job, being a big fish in Chicago, whereas it would be more difficult for him in New York. He liked being close to his family and friends in Wisconsin, and I wasn't near my family either way. I couldn't argue those points, but it broke my heart to think about not staying with the *Donahue* family. I reluctantly agreed to stay in Chicago, but because the job wasn't requiring a hard-and-fast answer yet, I didn't commit myself either way at work.

Now that we were engaged, I figured we would set the date and move forward with planning, but Andrew was in no hurry. I started to get some of the same old feelings deep in my gut that something was not right. Everything seemed a little more problematic than it should have been. I remember asking different friends who seemed to be in happy marriages, "How did you know it was right?" and they would always answer, "You just know." For the life of me, I didn't "just know." It seemed like we were trying way too hard to force our relationship to work.

As the summer progressed and all those who were moving were busily making their plans, I agonized over my decision to stay in Chicago. It was a familiar feeling: tormenting myself over something I wanted but Andrew didn't. We had been through so much, and now we were together . . . why was everything so difficult? As I prepared to move into my almost-completed Old Town townhouse, I thought at least I'd be living in a great place that would have been completely unaffordable in New York. But something was off between Andrew and me, and it created a fear inside me as I listened to my colleagues discussing where to live in Manhattan and what apartments they'd found.

One weekend toward the end of the summer, Andrew and I headed up to the Wisconsin lake where we would go to boat with friends and family. We spent a fun day waterskiing with his brother's family, and then we all headed out to dinner. When I excused myself to go to the ladies' room, Andrew's sister-in-law came with me. I loved Julie; we had an easy, comfortable, close relationship. Once inside the door, Julie turned to me.

"Lorri, I have to talk to you," she began. Her voice sounded serious, and my heart started thumping. Was there a problem between her and Andrew's brother? Was their baby sick? Andrew's mom or dad? "I've wanted to talk to you for a couple of weeks now, but I wanted to do it in person. I just can't keep quiet about this."

"Julie, you're scaring me," I murmured, not sure what was coming next.

"It's just that . . . well . . . I'm just going to say it," she stammered. "I'm so upset with Andrew, and I don't know how he can do this, and I think you deserve to know. He's cheating on you."

I stared at her wordlessly, my eyes wide open, my brain processing the bombshell she just dropped.

"He brought some girl up here!" she exclaimed. "I couldn't believe he would do this out in the open, not even trying to hide it. There's no way I wasn't going to tell you. For heaven's sake, you're engaged!"

As I listened to Julie go on about the injustice, Andrew's stupidity, and her inability to understand what he was doing, I inexplicably began to relax. In a matter of moments, I knew that I was finished with Andrew. Just like that.

"Julie, please don't worry about me," I told her. "You have just done me the greatest of favors. I can't tell you how much I appreciate the fact that you care enough to tell me the truth."

Julie hugged me and said vehemently, "I do care about you, and I care about him too, but what he's done to you is wrong. You can tell him I told you, too," she said assertively. "Please don't try to protect me. I don't care if he gets mad at me."

"Are you sure?" I asked cautiously. "You have to live with his brother, and I don't want to make life miserable for you."

"Absolutely," she said firmly. "Peter isn't too happy with him right now either. And you needed to know."

"Julie, you have no idea what you've done for me," I told her calmly. "Things have not been right between Andrew and me, but I haven't been able to face it or do anything about it. Aimee has always been here between us. She's either been a wedge or a magnet, and I could never quite pull away. Now I can."

Tears began to build in Julie's eyes. "I don't want to be the reason you two break up," she whispered.

I hugged her again, tightly. "Please believe me; you're not," I promised. "You have just given me what I needed in order to do what's long overdue. I can never, ever thank you enough."

I said nothing to Andrew about our conversation on the two-hour drive back to Chicago. I was mostly silent. My mind was filled with thoughts and feelings as I analyzed the news I'd received and what it meant. I certainly felt sadness and anger, but the unexpected overriding emotions were peace and resolution. It was over. Andrew had done the one thing I would never forget or get over, and it made what I had to do so much easier.

As we approached the city, Andrew began talking about an upcoming event and our plans for that night. I listened for a little while, then said calmly, "I talked to Julie today. She told me everything. She thought I should know you were seeing someone else. It makes breaking up a lot easier to take."

"What do you mean, breaking up?" Andrew questioned. "It's never been easy, not from the beginning. I'm sorry I did it, but I know I love you. We can work through this."

As we pulled up the drive to my apartment, I gathered my belongings. "I'm done working, Andrew," I said with a composure I felt through my whole body. For the first time, there was no angst, no stressful yin-yang feeling of being pulled in two directions. There was just that strange sense of relief. "It's not supposed to be such hard work," I said and turned to look at him full in the eyes. "We've tried over and over, and we just can't make it happen. This is something I won't just 'get through.' This is a dealbreaker. I'm done."

I got out of the car and leaned down, looking at Andrew. "It needed to be done, Andrew. You just made it a whole lot simpler to do it." I turned and walked away.

a new dawn

The next day, I told my boss I would be joining them in New York. There was no question in my mind, no further decision to be made. It felt right, and I knew there was nothing to keep me in Chicago anymore. Only one thought pricked at the back of my mind. For some reason, I assumed that Aimee was somewhere in Chicagoland or at least somewhere close. And although it didn't matter if I moved away, because I wasn't seeing her, I still felt a little bit like I was leaving her behind. I hadn't gotten any pictures or even another letter since The Cradle let me know that the records were open again, but somehow, I had a tough time reconciling the move. All the same, I had to figure it out, because I was going to New York.

A few days later, a call came into the office, and someone told me to pick it up.

"Hi, this is Carol Hadley Jones with CBS," said the voice on the other line. "I live in a one-bedroom in Manhattan at 57th and 8th Avenue on the 41st floor, and I've been transferred to DC. I heard about your show's move to New York, and I wondered if anyone there is looking for a sublet."

My ears immediately perked up. I had already taken my exploratory trip to New York in the spring and was now faced with the prospect of finding a place in a big hurry. It was like fate staring me in the face.

"Um, yes, as a matter of fact, I am," I told her, silently blessing the receptionist who had decided to send me this call. "Can you describe it to me?"

After five minutes on the phone with Carol, I took the apartment, sight unseen. I blanched at the price, a good five hundred dollars more a month than the mortgage on the townhouse I was moving into in two weeks, but the location was spectacular, and I could walk to work. Problem solved.

The next few weeks flew by. It seemed crazy to move to Old Town three months before moving to New York, but after the long, arduous process of building, I wanted to at least enjoy the place a little bit. It felt amazing to actually own my very first home, and I was determined to live in it, if only for a short time. I worked on getting all my ducks in a row in New York and then settled into appreciating and relishing my last few months in Chicago.

I called Jane at The Cradle and made sure she had both of my new addresses and my moving timetable so there would be no problem reaching me if a letter arrived. I wrote another letter to her and the board reiterating my points on allowing the adoptive parents and me to exchange letters and requesting any photographs that the adoptive family might send for me. Andrew called every couple of days, and at first, I didn't take his calls, but eventually, I picked up.

"Andrew, why are you calling?" I asked with purpose. I recognized the routine, but this time, I knew I needed to nip it in the bud.

"I just miss you and wanted to talk," he began. "Did you move into your townhouse? How is it? I'd love to come see it."

"Andrew, it's not going to happen," I said firmly. "Nothing is going to change this time, and I'm moving to New York in November."

He was silent for a few seconds. "So . . . you're moving?" he repeated. "I can't believe it. I can't believe you've made the decision to move so quickly."

"I made it the next day, Andrew," I informed him. "Really, this time, it's over."

The next day, a beautiful package arrived from the florist. I just shook my head when the burgeoning arrangement was placed on my desk, knowing what the card would read. It was as if Andrew was positive his usual tactics would once again bring me back to him, but this time, I knew it wasn't going to happen. I was truly and absolutely done, no looking back. I didn't even want to date anyone. I was not looking for someone to fill the void Andrew left. I was moving to New York, and the last thing I wanted was a man right now.

On October 25, 1984, less than six weeks before the move and about a month or two after Andrew and I broke up, I decided to stop in at an annual reunion for Miami University, my alma mater. Every year, it was held at a local bar on State Street, and this year, I figured I could say goodbye to any of my college friends who might show up. I was going to a movie screening anyway, and it was right on the way. I was having a great time catching up with friends when I noticed a familiar face walking in the door.

"Is that Steve Benson?" I asked my friend incredulously. In the eight years since college, Steve Benson had changed. His fraternity and my sorority had been social partners on many occasions, and he had been friends with a couple of my college boyfriends. I always liked his personality but never really thought of him as anything but a friend. The minute I saw him now, however, it was a completely different story. It was actually one of those "across a crowded room" kind of moments for me, and I made a beeline for the well-built, very handsome, grown version of the Steve Benson I'd known at Miami.

It turned out that Steve had just moved to Chicago and had come to the reunion to see who was in town from Miami. We immediately hit it off, and I felt a surprisingly strong connection almost instantly. When it was time to leave for the screening, I was disappointed but decided it was for the best. After all, I was moving in little more than a month!

The next day, my intercom rang at work.

"There's a Steve Benson on the line," the receptionist intoned. "Should I put him through?" *Steve Benson!!* My heart skipped a beat. How had he found me? My lips involuntarily formed a smile. "Absolutely," I answered.

We went to dinner and fell in love the same night. For the next five and a half weeks, we saw each other every night. It was simple, uncomplicated, and perfect. We were on the same page about everything, and we made each other laugh constantly. The only downside was the turning of the calendar pages as we got closer and closer to my moving date.

One night, I decided it was time to tell Steve about Aimee. This was such a huge thing in my life, and I wanted him to know the whole story. As I went through the saga, from beginning to end, his reaction was not what I expected. His eyes filled with tears for my loss, and he reached out to me and held me, allowing the dam inside me to open again. As I sobbed in new grief, three years after the fact, the knowledge that he not only understood but felt the

pain too meant more to me than I could ever express. There was no holding
back, no pulling away. He went through the photographs of Aimee, one by
one, taking his time, absorbed by each one. I immediately knew that he was
the right man for me.

Before we knew it, it was the *Donahue* show's last day in Chicago. I
had waved goodbye to the movers with all my belongings the day before
and given my new tenants the keys to my beloved townhouse. Steve and
I had decided to spend this last day together and then fly to Boca Raton,
Florida, for the week I had off work for the transition. Afterward, I would
fly to New York and he would come back to Chicago, and we would begin
a long-distance relationship. I had done a bad job of having nothing to do
with men, and suddenly I had the perfect guy and I didn't want to see it
end. With Steve, I did *just know*, like all those happy couples. With Steve,
it was easy and comfortable and magical. And now, we were going to live
in two different cities.

That morning, the final show was a blur of excitement. We had a big
farewell party in the offices afterward, and in the midst of the celebration,
someone called to me to pick up the phone. Andrew was in the lobby. I
glanced over at Steve, deep in conversation with one of my coworkers, and
didn't know how to respond to the guard. What was Andrew doing? We
hadn't spoken in several weeks. Finally, I told him I would come out.

Andrew stood there with a large, wrapped package.

"Andrew, what . . ." my sentence trailed off.

"I knew you were leaving," he broke in. "I just wanted to give you a
remembrance of Chicago and to say goodbye."

I stood there in surprise, certainly not expecting this. "I . . . Andrew, I
can't accept a gift. I'm leaving . . . it's over between us."

He paused a moment before answering. "I know you're leaving today.
Just leave it in the office if you don't want the gift, but I wanted to give it to
you and to wish you the best."

I was touched, but I knew that I was now involved with the right man.
"That's so thoughtful of you, but you should know I'm dating someone else
now, so you might want to hang onto the gift."

Andrew had heard that before, and it didn't phase him. "No, I want you
to have it, to remember all the good times in Chicago. And I just wanted to
see you before you left."

We spoke for a few moments and shared a small, awkward hug. With a wave, he went out the door, leaving me with the large, wrapped rectangle, which I carried back to the office. Steve came over immediately to ask where I went.

"Andrew came here," I said with a shake of my head. "He insisted on giving me this goodbye gift."

Steve, God bless him, without a hint of jealousy, said, "Well, open it. Let's see what it is!" I ripped open the package, and there was a very large, very beautiful framed photograph of Chicago, a lovely memento of a city that had indeed meant a lot to me.

Later that day, the entire staff and Phil's friends and family gathered at a large hotel suite at the Four Seasons for a final farewell. Steve and I were packed and ready to leave from there for our Boca Raton getaway. Steve found himself alone in the dining room with Marlo Thomas, who he'd met only on a couple of occasions.

"Marlo," he began tentatively, "so your man is coming to New York, and your commuting days are over. Lorri is the love of my life, and now we start commuting. Do you have any advice for me?"

Marlo's response was swift and certain. "Don't do it," she said firmly. "It was a long, terrible hardship. If you aren't sure and you're not ready to commit, just don't do it." The two spoke for a few more minutes, and then suddenly, it was time to catch our flight to Florida.

A few days later, we were walking hand in hand on the Boca beach, talking about life and when we'd see each other again. Suddenly, Steve very casually asked, "So when do you want to get married?"

I looked over at him curiously and said, half joking, "Is this a proposal?"

To my surprise, and a bit to his, he sank down to one knee and said, "I guess it is."

I never hesitated a second; there was no doubt in my mind. "There are two conditions," I said, smiling. "No beating, no cheating."

He stood up, wrapping his arms around me. "Done."

The next six months flew by. Steve and I picked May 25, 1985 for our wedding date—six months from the night we'd re-met. It took one conversation to decide that it would be better for Steve to move to New York for my job than for me to go back to Chicago for his. He had been considering switching to a career in finance and, coincidentally, had thought about trying for a job on Wall Street. This made it a no-brainer. We flew back and forth almost every weekend, and each visit made it clearer that we'd hit the lottery in each other.

Two months after the move, Andrew called my new office. When the intercom buzzed and I was told who was holding, I had a moment of panic, knowing this was most likely not going to be the easiest of chats.

"Hi, Andrew," I started out, and I decided to let him take the lead on the direction of the conversation. After catching up for a few minutes, he mentioned a potential trip to New York. Well, this was it. The moment of truth. "Andrew, I have some other news, too," I started and then just spit it out. "I got engaged about two months ago, and I'm getting married in May."

Silence. And then anger, followed by disbelief, accusations, and confusion. "How could this have happened so fast?" he asked incredulously. "Nobody gets engaged after a couple of weeks."

"Five and a half weeks, to be precise," I intoned quietly. "I know it's crazy fast, but it's absolutely the right thing for me." I can't say that I blamed him. I could hardly believe it myself, but I was listening to my gut, and my gut told me Steve would make me happy for the rest of my life.

In the meantime, I was slowly growing fonder of the Big Apple. At first, I was a little resentful that, for a lot more money, I'd left a nice, spacious, brand-new two-bedroom townhouse in Chicago for a small one-bedroom apartment in NYC, but I grew to appreciate the great location and the views from the 41st floor corner windows. It was thrilling to work at 30 Rock, and it was especially sweet that it was only a ten-minute walk from my apartment. It was so exciting to have a new studio and a new office, complete with a view overlooking 49th Street! This truly was the start of an adventure—a ride I never wanted to end.

By the time May 25 rolled around, I was marrying not only the love of my life but my best friend. There wasn't a doubt in my mind, and we both remember that day as one in which we had the time of our lives. Life settled into a blissful, newlywed dream of a routine. By the end of the summer, Steve had wrangled that job he wanted on Wall Street, and between his job and mine, every evening was a smorgasbord of opportunity. For a young dual-income couple, New York was most definitely the city that didn't sleep.

To make things even better, my letter to Aimee's adoptive mother over a year before had resulted in our ability to communicate through The Cradle indefinitely. With Jane's help, we had successfully circumnavigated the system and pried open our adoption just the tiniest bit. It certainly wasn't an open adoption, but after having nothing, it was something. The occasional letter from Aimee's mother or update from The Cradle was slow in coming, but after getting the first informative missive from her new mother, I was left with such a feeling of peace that I could finally relax just a little. Aimee was clearly with wonderful people, people I instinctively knew I would like immensely, people who loved her with a passion. For the first few years in New York, there was just enough information to keep the loss at bay—although none of the coveted pictures I needed and wanted. It seemed The Cradle board just didn't want to take any chances with the exchange of photographs. We could communicate via the occasional letter, but pictures were not part of the deal.

For the most part, I was living the dream, and I felt lucky to be living it with my soul mate. I took nothing for granted. Also, for the most part, I was reconciled with Aimee and her life. Every now and then, however, I suffered the occasional period of anguish, usually after reading an article, watching a movie, or, sometimes, receiving an update, but more time began to elapse between moments of mourning. Certainly, the passage of time had something to do with healing the wound, but it was also partly due to my changing life and to the fact that I had, quite literally, moved on. I was in a new city and a blessedly happy marriage, and our life together was full, exciting, and a great adventure. Andrew called occasionally, and although he had understandably been shocked and upset to hear how quickly I'd altered my marital status, we ended up redefining the friendship which had started our whole relationship saga. Aimee would always be a link for us, and, over the years, we would catch up every now and then, especially after letters or updates on Aimee.

Work was challenging, invigorating, and amazing. New York brought a new energy to our audiences and easy access to all the best guests. The marketplace was getting crowded, mostly with competitors who pushed the edge of the tabloid television envelope, and we responded sometimes in kind but mostly by digging deeper for the newsmakers and taking the show on location, directly to the viewers and to exciting milieus.

Steve and I hadn't quite reached our eight-month anniversary when I realized, once again, that I had no issues with fertility. Without trying to get pregnant, and even while using my worthless diaphragm, I found myself, once again, wondering what happened to my period. This time, however, that aha moment produced a very different reaction from my partner and me.

"Sooooo, I have something to tell you," I said teasingly to Steve one night after work, and I handed him an envelope. Inside was a card with a pregnant belly on the front with pink and blue baby shoes balanced on it.

"Oh, a mysterious secret?" he laughed, ripping open the envelope. I watched his face as he read the card. We hadn't even reached our first anniversary yet, and when we talked about children, we'd thought it would be a couple of years down the line. We were having the time of our lives exploring life as a young newlywed couple. I waited, watching for a ripple of disappointment or frustration to cross his face. Instead, I saw pure joy and excitement.

"Whaaat! Are you sure?" he exclaimed. "That's incredible!" He reached over and grabbed me, pulling me into a huge hug.

"Oh, I'm so glad you're happy!" I started tearing up. "I have to go to the doctor, but I'm pretty positive. I wasn't sure how you would react . . . it's SO much sooner than we planned, and we're having such a great time, just the two of us."

He pulled away just long enough to look at me like I was crazy. "Are you kidding? Okay, maybe it's coming faster than we'd first decided, but I guess it's not always our decision. A baby? It's fantastic!"

I looked at him wryly. "I'm apparently not great at this birth control thing."

We both laughed, and then Steve got a little serious. "Honey, how are you feeling about this, you know . . . with Aimee, and all that?"

I looked at him and didn't think I could love him more. "Yes, well, I have to admit, it's brought up a lot of emotions . . . a lot of memories . . . and it's made me miss her," I admitted quietly. "But the idea of having our baby . . . well, for me, I couldn't be happier."

"That makes two of us," he said, squeezing me tighter.

The month before our baby was born, I reached out to The Cradle. We had just bought a house down near the shore in New Jersey, and I wanted to give them the new address, but, more importantly, I needed an update. Too much time had passed. I gave Jane the address and then gave her my news.

Steve and I are expecting our first child around the end of September, and if the adoptive parents are interested, I'd like for them to know that. Somehow, I feel they would be happy to know that things have worked out for me.

I asked for details on her development, how was she getting along with her sister, and were there plans for a larger family? What kinds of activities was she exposed to, and were there any early tendencies toward any talents? I apologized for all my questions and thanked Jane for her proactiveness on my behalf. And, of course, I did just have to put one more plug in for pictures.

I would like to state once again my desire for any photographs, with her adoptive parents' consent, of course. Should there be any changes concerning that decision, I would certainly like to know.

Cordially,

Lorri Antosz Benson

baby steps

Taryn Leigh entered our lives on September 25, 1986. Staring down at our perfect, beautiful daughter, I was overcome with a blissful contentment I'd never known before. This is what I'd missed with Aimee: this connection, this magic allowed to fully develop in a sweet, intoxicating blend of wonder, awe, and joy. A tear slowly streaked down my cheek as I mourned my firstborn child while simultaneously rejoicing in Steve's and my incredible miracle. As my tiny daughter nursed with all her might, I slowly reconciled the feelings of loss and began to focus on the overwhelming maternal bond of protectiveness and love I felt for the small being in my arms.

I received a response from Jane six months later. She explained that they had to wait for the family to voluntarily contact them and then they would forward my request for more information. If the adoptive family reached out, they would let me know and send the letter. If I reached out to them, The Cradle had to wait for the adoptive family to contact them before sending my letter. It seemed backwards to me, but I was in no position to argue. In addition, their policy on the exchange of photos had not changed but continued to be a topic of discussion.

Hmmph. A topic of discussion. While you all are discussing, I'm trying to picture this child, trying to put a face on the little girl I'm imagining as I read this update.

And that was the good part. There was another update.

She started kindergarten this fall and enjoys it thoroughly . . . When she begins first grade, the parents have chosen to send her to a Catholic grade school. Her parents describe her as very bright and exceptionally verbal and dramatic. She is taking ballet lessons this year, and the family feels this will be good for her physical development. She also enjoys the classes. The parents relate that while their daughters have very different personalities, they get along well and have a very warm sibling relationship.

This family continues to do very well and is just as enthusiastic about being parents as they were at placement time. The husband has had employment opportunities that would require relocation, but he has turned them down because he feels strongly that the environment they are in now has more positives for their family. Both girls are close to their grandparents, and relocation would put limits on extended family relationships.

While this letter can in no way express the love and devotion these parents have for their daughters, be assured that Aimee continues to develop well in a very secure and loving family. I'm sure your life has changed dramatically since the birth of your child in the fall. I hope everything went smoothly for you and that your family is happy and healthy.

Sincerely,

Jane

As the months turned into years, I realized a lot of things. I quickly learned that one child does not substitute for another. I'd read stories about parents who had lost a child to illness or accidents and then had another baby, and they always mentioned that they weren't trying to replace the first child, because it was impossible to do that. I learned firsthand the truth of that statement. Having Taryn did not make me forget about Aimee. In many ways, it made me think of her more often, wondering if Aimee had started walking at that age or talking as early as Taryn did. At the same time, though, it did fill the void. Taryn was a gift, and mothering her fulfilled the maternal longing I had inside. I loved being a mom.

Another thing I learned is that it is not very easy to take a baby to work. I took Phil up on his very generous offer to bring Taryn with me to work whenever I wanted. I was the only one in the office with a very young child, and given that my demanding work schedule was part of the reason I relinquished Aimee in the first place, I felt compelled to bring Taryn with me as often as possible. Not wanting to raise a baby in the city, we had moved to the suburbs a month before Taryn was born. After an idyllic six-month maternity leave, Steve's sister helped out until we hired Liz, a fantastic Irish nanny. Bringing Taryn into the office meant packing up equipment, paraphernalia, necessities, diaper bag, and baby, all accompanied by our nanny. There was no way I would get anything done at work without Liz. I would hold Taryn and then hand her back to go to a meeting. Then hold her and hand her back to take a phone call. Anyone who has tried this knows it's almost impossible to be fully productive and have your baby at work.

And it wasn't that this was so great for Taryn. She napped in a port-a-crib I kept in my office, went on walks around 30 Rock, and ate her meals at the conference table. I'm sure she would have been just fine in her own bed in our comfortable home in New Jersey, and I know Liz and most of the staff would have preferred that too. I blessed Phil for allowing what for the most part was an indulgence to make me feel less guilty.

I continued to learn what an amazing job, and boss, I had. Five years after the trip to France, Phil announced we would celebrate the twenty-year anniversary of the show with a trip to the Italian, French, and Spanish Rivieras aboard the *Sea Goddess*, a small, intimate luxury cruise liner. Phil had chartered not only the entire ship but also the *Concorde* to ferry us across the pond. Steve and I were over the moon; who wouldn't be? We made arrangements for Taryn, and although it was tough to be away from our daughter, it was an implausibly amazing and romantic getaway.

I also learned that a picture is worth a thousand words, or maybe ten thousand. When Taryn was about a year old and Aimee was six years old, I got a letter from The Cradle. It had been six months since I'd had a letter or update, but this note said they had something from Aimee's adoptive mother, and would I want them to forward it? Why did they keep asking that question? I had told them after the last letter to just send me anything from the adoptive parents. Impatiently, I picked up the phone and once more told Jane to please send this and ANY correspondence directly to me, no delay, no questions asked. I impatiently waited for the interminable time it took the US Post Office to get the letter to me. Finally, five days later, the envelope arrived. I ripped it open, and two photographs slipped out. TWO PICTURES. I held the photos as though they were delicate flowers that might disintegrate under my touch. I had prayed that I might someday see Aimee's face, but I couldn't imagine how surreal it would feel. The adorable child I stared at was at different ages in each picture. I opened the letter and read the explanation.

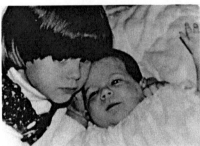

Aimee/Katie, age 3 1/2, with her sister, Mary Ellen

Aimee/Katie, age 5 1/2, with her sister, Mary Ellen

The Cradle board had finally decided we could exchange photographs! My heart was racing out of control as I realized that what I'd been fighting for all these years was actually happening. It turns out that Aimee's adoptive mother had sent a photo when she was three and again at five—the photos I now held in my hands. On the one hand, I was furious that they had been kept from me after Aimee's mom had expressly sent them for me. On the other hand, I couldn't be mad because I WAS LOOKING AT MY BIRTHDAUGHTER! After six long years, I was finally gazing at her sweet face. She looked a lot like Andrew, but I could see a little of me and a little of Taryn in her.

When Steve got home, he found me staring at the two pictures. "What's that? What are you looking at?"

I looked up at him with red eyes and tears of happiness drying on my face. "Aimee," I whispered. "They sent pictures of Aimee."

He sucked in his breath, sat down, and reached for the photos. As he studied her dark eyes, small straight nose, and lovely brown hair, he murmured, "She's beautiful, Lorri, just beautiful. I know what this means to you . . . it's amazing."

I watched my husband gazing at the pictures with the same interest and the same tug of emotion as I had and said another silent prayer of thanks that he had somehow been brought into my life. He just got it.

I learned that time does somehow heal all wounds. Andrew came to New York on a business trip and asked me to come to lunch, just to catch up. The day arrived, and we sat down at a casual place near Rockefeller Center. After we had caught up on most of our news, I decided to tell him what I'd saved for last.

"So, there is one more thing," I said, pausing a moment. "It's been six years, and I just got two pictures of Aimee." I glanced at him and watched his eyes widen and his mouth open. "She's three and a half in one picture and five and a half in the other. I have them with me if you'd like to see them." Andrew stared at me. I didn't expect him to say yes; after all, he'd still never seen her pictures from the three days in the hospital. But he surprised me.

"Yeah, I would," he said slowly. He sat looking at them for what seemed like a lifetime. When he looked up, I saw the tears on his cheeks. I immediately felt an emotional release, and the two of us sat crying, the pictures between us. It was a touching, poignant moment, perhaps the most moving five minutes of our long and tumultuous relationship. When it was time to go, we hugged affectionately. We'd had a tough journey together and had gone our separate ways, but there would always be a connection through Aimee.

I sent a thank you to Jane and the board to let them know how important these pictures were.

> *Dear Jane and board members,*
>
> *As much as this is your life's work, I wonder if you will ever know how much the pictures mean to me. As I stated in a previous letter, Aimee is, and will always be, in my thoughts. Rather than serving as a reminder, the photos satisfy something inside which aches with curiosity and the desire to know her. This helps. This is cathartic for me.*
>
> *I know your wish is to try to make difficult situations a little better and brighter for all. You have done this for me by changing this aspect of your policy, and I encourage this type of openness and flexibility in the future . . . I know you don't control the inflow of correspondence from her adoptive parents, but I anxiously await the arrival of more photos and information about Aimee. By the way, Andrew visited me recently, and I showed him the photos. It was emotional, but very comforting for him as well, and he shares my excitement at having these pictures . . .*
>
> *Cordially,*
>
> *Lorri Antosz Benson*

I needed to thank Aimee's adoptive parents too. Their willingness to share their life with me was astounding, and I needed them to know how grateful I was.

Dear Parents,

. . . I'm not sure if you know this, but until recently, The Cradle's policy was not to exchange photos, and I didn't receive the photos of her at age three and a half and five and a half until a couple of months ago . . . I have longed for a photo to satisfy the ever-present curiosity about how she has physically changed from the baby pictures I have and what she looks like now. Out of the blue, the pictures arrived, and she is everything I have dreamed.

I wanted to let you know how precious these photos are to me and how much I appreciate your openness and confidence in sending them, as well as the updates you've sent in the past. I want you to know, as always, you have nothing to fear from me. These pictures reassure me that although that difficult decision will always be with me, this child is loved and well cared for by a wonderful, compassionate couple.

I don't know if this will ever come to pass, but if someday we are destined to meet, and I pray we are, I hope to be able to express to you the level of appreciation which I feel. Until then, I hope you will continue to feel comfortable sending photos and information to me. They mean so much.

Love,

Aimee's Birthmother

One last thing that I learned during this time was that Phil Donahue was finding it super hard to leave his very challenging but rewarding job, and I knew how he felt. I had been promoted to Senior Producer, and by the time we decided to have a second child (yes, decided), I had begun to feel like there weren't enough hours in the day or fuel in my tank to do everything I needed to do. I was heavily influenced by the feminist leanings of my boss and the women's movement leaders who frequented the media, including our stage, and I WAS going to *have it all*. I discovered, however, that having it all was exhausting, especially when it included being second in command of a leading national talk show, being pregnant while having a two-year-old, and having a three-hour round-trip commute. I went to Phil and reluctantly told him my tenure and energy level might be coming to an end.

"Wait, wait, wait." He waved me into a seat. As I eased my hugely pregnant self into a chair, he outlined his plan to quit at the end of his current contract in 1992. "Just stay with me until the end," he asked, "and we'll go out together. It won't be that much longer, just a few years." He went on to suggest I bring both children in whenever I wanted, and although I cringed at the thought of a crying infant and lively two-year-old taking over the office, I loved him for proposing it. Steve and I discussed keeping the current pace up and decided to try to move either back to the city or closer to it so we could at least gain back some of the three hours we spent commuting. We put our house on the market, and when our darling Taylor made her entrance in April 1989, I had another six months off to fortify me. We couldn't justify live-in help during this time, so wonderful Liz left to pursue new quests, and when my leave ended, equally wonderful Cecily came to take her place.

Turns out, it was, unfortunately, a terrible housing market, and try as we might, we could not sell our house unless we were willing to take a huge loss. We took it off the market after about eighteen months, unsure of what our next step should be. Life was still wild and crazy, made even more so with a second child. Cecily was a blessing from heaven, and we managed to keep things at a status quo, juggling a million balls in the air while enjoying our time with our young family.

The show went on summer hiatus each year, and although we still came to the office, mostly to clean out and prepare for the new fall season, we had relaxed hours, and bringing the girls in to work was not as invasive. At least it felt that way . . . my colleagues were too kind to say anything otherwise.

Steve and I made the decision that we needed to leave New York and move somewhere where we could live a lifestyle completely involved in our children's lives. We saw countless older men and women on our commutes, people who had spent their lives on the trains or highways, and we knew that wasn't the life we wanted if we could help it. The questions were when and where we would go and what we would do. When it was clear our plan to move back to the city was not going to materialize any time soon, we spent hours running the pros and cons of staying through Phil's contract, and we decided to keep all the balls in the air for a little while longer.

Aimee's parents and I exchanged letters, and little by little, we got to know each other better. I tried to keep The Cradle up to date on everything going on in my life, just in case, especially since we exchanged our letters through the agency. I figured you just didn't know what the future held, and I wanted all the cards to be on the table. In 1990, I told Jane about our crazy but wonderful life with two children and our attempt to balance everything. I also updated her on Andrew.

I stay in touch with Aimee's father, Andrew. We are still very friendly, much friendlier than when we were together, I might add. He has, in the last two and a half years, married and produced a sixteen-month-old son and a two-month-old daughter. He lives in a Chicago suburb and is also very interested in updates about Aimee. Anything you send to me will be copied and forwarded to him.

I reiterated my usual request for more photos and added that I would be more than willing to meet Aimee and her family if she ever desired such a meeting. A few months later, I received a request that brought both waterworks and a smile to my face.

Dear Lorri,

The worker for Aimee's adoptive family said that the adoptive parents would be very interested in having an updated letter written by you that they would be able to share with Aimee when appropriate. They would hope you could share information about yourself and your family, and information about the birthfather would also be welcome.

Obviously they have all the non-identifying information that was originally shared and your letter from the time of placement. They feel just knowing how things are going for you now would be helpful to have as Aimee has new questions . . .

Sincerely,

Jane

Wow. This was the first time there was a request from Aimee's family for more information about me. Up until this time, it had always been me doing the appeals. My heart raced. My birthdaughter was asking questions. She wanted to know more. And her amazing parents were giving her as much information as she needed. They were not minimizing her requests; in fact, just the opposite. They were going the extra mile, asking for more openness, more honesty. They wanted her to know about me! With joy and hope, I wrote a letter without identifiable names or places but one that described my life, my expanding family, and, as always, my never-ending love for Aimee. I sent it off to The Cradle and imagined Aimee and her parents sitting together, reading about me, Steve, and our girls.

In return, The Cradle forwarded several letters from her mother over the next two years: long, handwritten missives on yellow legal pad paper. She freely shared the particulars of their life together. She wrote about Aimee's academics, her sports, her friends, and her relatives. She was clearly smitten with "our" daughter, as she called her.

Dear Birthmother,

I guess I can't stop saying good things about this precious daughter—she's really quite beautiful inside and out. We've had our fair share of normal disciplinary flaps—she was in the terrible twos as far as the strong will goes 'til about age five, but with each passing year, it gets easier to reason with her, and she's maturing in her attitudes and behavior. She is surrounded by love—school, home, family, and friends—so she's happy, secure, and self-confident.

When she was about six years old, she started asking about you. The first night we talked about you, she seemed upset at the prospect of not knowing you. We told her as much as we could, particularly how much you loved her to let us be her parents. She seems to accept that and whenever she's troubled, she has a long chat with her dad, who is also adopted . . . I will never know exactly how she feels about it, but she doesn't seem to be adversely affected. The process has brought us so much joy—I can't help but think that spills over to her.

She talked about Aimee's relationships with her obviously wonderful dad, her sister, her grandparents. And then she wrapped it up.

I guess I've talked about everyone but me and our daughter. I've probably avoided that because it might cause you some hurt to hear details of the relationship you gave to me. Just know that I feel so very lucky to have her, and I'll do everything in my power to protect her and prepare her for what I hope will be a happy and fulfilling adult life. I thank God for you and for her.

Most sincerely,

Our Daughter's Mother

I would always cry. I guess I would have cried in any case because it was so emotional to learn new things about this daughter I didn't know. But I also cried because this woman was so loving and so giving, not only to our daughter but to me. She signed her letters "Our Daughter's Mother"—her capacity to love amazed me. Another letter focused on their gentle attempts to guide Aimee through the minefield of learning her adoption story.

September 20, 1990

> *Dear Birthmother,*
>
> *. . . It was wonderful to hear of your family and your happiness, and we loved the pictures. It's both exciting and unreal to think that Aimee has two more sisters. Maybe one day, she can meet them.*

My heart stood still. SHE was wishing they could meet? SHE would help facilitate a meeting? Hope sprang from every pore in my body.

> *Aimee and I have discussed the adoption laws and procedure, and she knows that once she is of a certain age (I never can remember if it's eighteen or twenty-one), she can request disclosure, and upon mutual request, it will be made by The Cradle. I have not pushed in either direction. I feel that is such a personal decision for her and one that's still years away.*

Okay, well, years away. I supposed that made sense. And while I understood and agreed with her approach of not pushing either way, I'll admit I kind of was wishing she'd push a little bit for disclosure.

> *In the interim, Aimee has what seems to be a very matter-of-fact approach. She's occasionally curious, and I give her pretty much whatever information she asks about. When we picked her up from The Cradle, we were given a poop sheet on you and her birthfather. She has seen them and knows where to look in the file cabinet. She even remarked recently that she must have a pretty good bit of Italian genes because she loves Italian food so much.*

She went on to say that she'd not shared my initial letter with her because her little sister's birthmother had no contact at all with her. She was worried it could hurt the little sister and felt Aimee needed to be a little older to have that information.

> *Rest assured that there will come a time when we feel that we can give Aimee your letter from November 1981 and any others. I hate keeping them from her, but I think it will all work out in a few months or years . . .*
>
> *Love,*
>
> *Aimee's Mom and Dad*

It was a full update and a letter that truly gave me the courage to dream that more was to come. For the longest time, I prayed only for photos and information. Now I wondered: was it possible that the future might hold a relationship for not only Aimee and me but also for her two mothers?

revisiting grief

About this time, Steve and I had a heart to heart about a third child. Life was just about as full as we could handle, but somehow, we both felt a powerful tug for one more, and we decided we liked the two-to-three-year age difference. Maybe we were gluttons for punishment, but we did the math and planned it out, and, once again, the fertility gods smiled on us. Taylor would be two and a half when the new baby was born, and our family would be complete. We decided that would be a perfect time to make our transition to our new life.

That's when we learned that life really is about peaks and valleys. After three textbook pregnancies, it never occurred to me that there could ever be a problem. I was in my fifth month when I went to the doctor for a regular monthly visit. The second trimester was always fun, and this one had been just like the first three . . . no issues. The nurse began all the initial prep—taking vitals and listening to heartbeats.

Except she couldn't find the baby's heartbeat.

"I'm sure it's just me," she muttered, shaking her head. "The baby is probably hiding behind an organ or something." After a good two minutes of moving the doppler from place to place, she finally said, "Oh, there it is," and got me ready for Dr. Al.

Dr. Al was the best. He literally LOVED his job and seemed in awe of the miracles he saw every day. But there was no miracle for me that day. He came in and gave me a hug and asked how things were going.

"Um, I know this is silly, but could you check the baby's heartbeat?" I felt like a Nervous Nellie, but just couldn't stop the uneasy feeling I had. "The nurse had a lot of trouble finding it, and then when she said she found it, it just sounded weird to me," I explained.

Dr. Al bent over my little baby bump with the doppler. Like the nurse, he moved the instrument all around my stomach for several minutes. Unlike the nurse, when he stopped, he had a serious look on his face.

"Okay, I'm having trouble finding the heartbeat," he admitted. "But I want you to listen to me. This has happened many times, and everything turns out to be just fine. I don't want you to panic or jump to conclusions."

But I was already beginning to shut down. I knew it was over. I listened to him tell me that they were setting up an ultrasound around the corner, and I was to go as soon as Steve could get there.

That sentence confirmed my fears. He wanted Steve to be with me. He knew there was something very, very wrong. He was just trying to keep me calm. I picked up the phone and called Steve. The instant I heard his voice, I began to crumble.

"It's me," I whispered tearfully. "You need to come meet me at Dr. Al's."

He immediately was attuned to my unspoken intent. "What is it, honey; what's wrong?"

"They can't find the heartbeat," I cried. "Dr. Al says it might be just fine, but I have to go get an ultrasound." I didn't tell him that I knew deep in my gut that our baby was gone.

"Don't move," he ordered. "I am getting a car and leaving this minute. Just wait there." He took a breath and then added, "Everything will be fine. I love you," and hung up.

I began to pace back and forth in the small room. This could not be happening. I felt like I was watching a movie that had suddenly taken a terrible turn. I picked up the phone and called my office, asking for my boss, the executive producer.

"Pat, I . . . I . . ." No words would form. I tried again. "Pat, um . . . something's wrong." She quietly got the story out of me, told me everything would be fine, and said to take all the time I needed. I walked out of the exam room and bumped right into Dr. Al.

"Did you reach Steve?" he asked. "Is he on his way?" As I nodded slowly, not able to make eye contact, he grabbed me by the shoulders. "Lorri, this could turn out just fine. Don't give up hope. I'm sure the baby's just in a bad position." He handed me a piece of paper with the address of the ultrasound lab and gave me a hug. "I'll see you after the test," he promised.

I walked to the lobby and felt like all eyes were on me. I felt like everyone knew, like everyone was staring at me, feeling sorry for me. I couldn't stand it. I half-ran to the door and burst outside. I remember it was a spectacularly beautiful day. *How could this happen? I've already lost one baby; please, God, don't let me lose another one.* I walked down to the corner, then back to the doctor's office. I began to pace up and down the block, rubbing my stomach and trying to push away the feelings of despair. *When was the last time I felt the baby move?* As I made a lap back down the street, Steve suddenly rounded the corner ahead of me at a fast run. He saw me and sprinted the distance to me, throwing his arms around me.

"Honey, we'll be okay," he vowed. "We will get through this. And the baby will be okay."

I looked up at his terrified face . . . sweat dripping down his brow. I couldn't tell him what I instinctively already knew.

Losing Aimee was one kind of pain: drawn out, dull, and throbbing. The loss of this baby was another: sudden and piercing. When the ultrasound confirmed that there was no heartbeat and that our baby was gone, I entered a fog of desolation. I remember Dr. Al quietly walking me through the next steps, getting me ready for the next day's events, which would render me un-pregnant. I remember the drive home after the ultrasound in the back of a town car, Steve and I clinging to each other, both unable to comprehend the turn our lives had taken. He was a rock, though . . . solid, supportive, and, at least for my benefit, optimistic that we would manage this crisis.

We did . . . somehow, but it took time. It was a shocking loss, and when the test results came back, it was even more shattering. All the tests, including chromosome studies, were normal. The conclusion was that it was a cord entanglement: a terrible accident that took the life of a healthy baby boy. Losing him brought back a lot of the feelings of emptiness and devastation I experienced with Aimee's adoption, but this time, I had two children and a loving husband and staying mired in sorrow was not a choice. Having a partner who mourned with me and who had no agenda but my happiness went a long way toward healing the wounds.

About six weeks later, at Phil's Christmas party, my boss announced the plans for the big 25th anniversary celebration for the next fall. It was mind-blowing. There would be a primetime TV special for the occasion, we would produce a compilation episode showcasing all the highlights from the last two-and-a-half decades, and, of course, there would be a trip. But not just any trip. Phil stood in front of the staff in his living room on Fifth Avenue.

"This is a big milestone," he began, while everyone waited on pins and needles. You could practically hear the room hum with anticipation. "I've decided we need to celebrate with something special." He went on to outline an actual trip around the world. It would include our very own chartered L-1011, outfitted to fit our group entirely in first-class accommodations. We would spend a day in Ireland, the land of the Donahue heritage. Then we would head east, refuel in Bahrain, and arrive in Bangkok. After a couple of days in Thailand, we would board our chartered luxury *Sea Goddess* to explore Indonesia, Bali, Singapore, and, finally, Hong Kong. From there, we would board our plane again, stop in Hawaii, and then head home, having circled the globe. It was a trip we couldn't even imagine in our wildest dreams. It gave us something truly amazing to anticipate, and we began looking forward to it on our drive home following the party.

The urge for a third child became imperative. Where once it was a discussion, we now both innately knew we had to have a third child. We waited about nine months and then proactively began trying. And all we wanted was a healthy child. The last time, on a lark, we had followed the advice of a book that had crossed my desk on how to choose the sex of your child by timing, eating certain foods, taking temperatures, etc., and it had resulted in a boy that we lost. That experience had given me a taste of the disappointment adoptive parents who were unable to conceive went through. This time, we couldn't have cared less what sex the baby was. We had realized that the only thing that mattered was a healthy baby carried to term. When we went on the trip around the world, I was the exact number of weeks through my fifth pregnancy as when we lost our son. It was unnerving. We took nothing for granted this time and had none of the breezy confidence that accompanied the first four pregnancies. We had learned firsthand that the worst really could happen.

Meanwhile, Phil's contract ended, and much to my shock and surprise, he renewed it! Of course, he had all his personal reasons to renew, and it really was not about me, but it had a huge effect on my family and me. Pregnant for the fifth time, anticipating my third baby, and still living over an hour from the city, I was completely overwhelmed with the idea of continuing this life-style. Steve and I hunkered down to discuss our options and decided we just couldn't continue the juggling act. It was time to transition to something different. When I told Phil, he once again launched into his song and dance about retiring after this new contract. He was nothing if not persuasive; Phil could make *Naked and Afraid* sound like a picnic in Central Park. I left his office thinking maybe we could figure it out.

Meanwhile, Jane had left her position at The Cradle, and I began getting updates and information from new people. I missed the personal connection I'd had with Jane. I had felt like I had a friend at The Cradle looking out for me. She knew my story. She had cared about me at a time when I really needed someone, and I was sorry to have her leave my life. She had apparently schooled her replacement well, though, and by this time, our kind of semi-open situation was becoming more accepted. Although all correspondence went through The Cradle, I received letters and detailed information from Aimee's mother as Aimee grew by leaps and bounds. While never enough, I appreciated every letter.

When our third and last child, Halli, was born, we were over the moon. There were four years between her and Taylor, which turned out to be a wonderful spread. With Taryn, everything was new and unknown, and I realized later that I had been a little hard on myself. I strived for perfection in everything, not realizing that perfection is overrated, especially when you're learning with no manual or training wheels. With Taylor, I also had a two-year-old, so life was crazy busy. When Halli arrived, I had both experience and two relatively independent children. I savored her infancy and enjoyed every second of the five months I had off work. I went back to the show at the end of September 1993, and some Fridays, I would come in with Cecily and *three* little girls. It was a circus. My office looked like a daycare center. I was so happy to have them there, though, because now that Taryn was in real school and Taylor in preschool, there were more Fridays than not that I couldn't bring them in.

I wasn't sure when all this had happened, but I'd suddenly gone from being the youngest employee to the matriarch with three kids. In New York, we hired a younger group of producers, and as my family responsibilities grew at home, I had less and less energy to give at the office. When I'd leave at six o'clock on the dot to catch my six thirty train, I sensed resentment or maybe disdain from some of my younger colleagues who would be in the office until all hours. I didn't blame them. I knew this job was all-consuming, and I'd been in their shoes. Now I wasn't giving anything in my life 100 percent, but I also knew that even by catching that six-thirty train, I still wouldn't get home until eight o'clock at night, and I'd have one precious hour with my babies at most. Phil, the father of five, understood my position and never complained about my waning devotion. But a great part of my angst that newer staff members didn't process, or even know, was the constant reminder that one of the reasons I relinquished Aimee was to provide her with full-time parents. Now, here I was, juggling my life. I needed and wanted more time with our girls, and I loved my job. It was too much, and I had to choose.

As much as I wanted to stay with Phil until the end of the show, I had to stop the merry-go-round. In February 1994, Steve left his job and began the transition of starting his own business, and in May, after almost fifteen years, I finally and tearfully left the *Donahue* show. Halli was a year old and Aimee almost thirteen. Phil and I, and many of the staff, had been through a lot together. We had been family. In true form, Phil and Marlo threw a fantastic farewell party at their home in Connecticut, complete with memorable and generous gifts and a loving acceptance of my reality.

Five months later, we relocated our young family to Naples, Florida, a place most of my New York friends couldn't fathom living. "What will you do? Who will you talk to? Where will you shop?" were just a few of the questions we heard from people who couldn't imagine living anywhere but the Big Apple. I had no answers but a lot of hope. We had no secure jobs, three children, and a finite savings account. What could go wrong?

first light

Steve set up his business as a planned giving specialist while I set up our family and began looking for work that I could do from home. I greatly missed Phil and my friends at *Donahue*, but I loved being home with the girls and having the flexibility to help at school and call my own hours. As much as New York had gotten in my blood, when Steve and I were sitting on the beach late every Friday afternoon, watching the girls play in the waves and sand while we watched the sunset with wine and appetizers, I never looked back. Sharing these simple, relaxed evenings together with our family was why we moved, and somehow, we would make this work.

It wasn't easy. Starting your own business never is, and Steve was starting from scratch. He spent the first year developing relationships and making his presence known. He loved being president of his own company, having the freedom to come and go as he pleased, and he took naturally to entrepreneurship. I, on the other hand, was just short of wailing and gnashing of teeth as I watched our savings dip lower and lower. I couldn't sit still and began putting irons in the fire for jobs that could be done primarily from home. Before too long, I was writing a syndicated column about the talk show scene and executive-producing a local talk show, *Golden Lifestyles*. I also did freelance writing for magazines and other producing, including doing some TV pilots in India.

No one was happier than me when Steve's business finally took off and I could stop stressing and focus more on just writing and being a mom. I began to think about writing a book on my adoption story.

In 1995, as our life settled down in Florida, a large package from The Cradle arrived. My hands were shaking as I showed Steve what was in the mail. Was it possible? Could this dream I never allowed myself to imagine really happen? For once, The Cradle hadn't sent a letter asking permission to send correspondence from Aimee's parents. I found myself realizing that there was something to the idea of preparing somebody for something so monumental. I grabbed scissors to open the package and quickly did the math—Aimee was an implausible thirteen! How did the time pass so quickly?

I turned the package upside down; three letters and a large packet dropped out. What was all this? I saw The Cradle stationary, so I ripped that open first.

The enclosed letters and photographs arrived for you from your birthdaughter and her adoptive parents.

I dropped the letter and screamed. Like clockwork, the tears came. What to look at first? I hesitated momentarily, wanting to read my daughter's words. But pictures . . . to see her . . . the two pictures I'd gotten so far were received seven years before. I just couldn't wait.

Steve looked over my shoulder as I examined every detail in each photo, one by one. There were nineteen in all, and it took a good hour to devour the bunch. Aimee . . . from age nine through thirteen with her sister and her grandparents, during the holidays and in dance recitals, playing in the snow and on the beach. It was a smorgasbord of Aimee, and my photo-starved eyes couldn't get enough. We laughed and cried as we looked at each photo again and again, and I memorized every expression, every feature.

Then it was time to turn to the two remaining letters, one from Aimee and one from her adoptive mom. I picked up the delicate pink envelope, which was the thinner of the two. *Birth Mom* was written on the front. Why was she writing? What would her first words to me be? I was shaking with the emotion of the moment. I tore it open. With her adolescent penmanship, my daughter asked me certain questions about the circumstances of her birth, but not really the all-important question: *why*. Perhaps that would come later. She told me about her life. I read quickly and hungrily. It was as though all the planets and stars had lined up to make things perfect.

Dear Birth Mom,

I don't know how to start this letter. I don't even know who to address it to, but of course you know that I know about the letters, and my adoptive parents have not kept anything from me. I have not read the letters, and I don't know if I will. I really appreciate your concern for me, and I worry because my sister, who is also adopted, does not receive (or rather my parents don't) any correspondence. I find it hard to think that there is someone out there that is my "real" mother because I love my parents and they love me, and I have never known anyone else. I do know that there is someone out there that loved me enough to give me to capable parents. I think I understand why in the most basic sense, but I realize that I will never fully know. I know that there is someone out there who cared about my life and the lives of other unborns not to have an abortion. In knowing that, I say that I want you to write your book about your experiences. I want the world to see that the adoption process can be a blessing. Our story is not an uncommon one, but it is a story that should be much, much more common. I know many people whom the adoption process has been a blessing to. I wish that every child could have a home that loves them.

About me, well, I am thirteen. I love to dance, act, read, write, ski, shop, talk, and surf the Internet. I hate sunburn, sickness, anger, fighting, and seeing hurt—whether physical, mental, or spiritual. I have two pen pals. One lives in Switzerland, and the other is my best friend who recently moved to Australia. I am hoping to have a third—Prince William. I am writing a letter to him and hoping for a response!

Love always,

Your Daughter

I began to laugh, simply in pure joy. As Steve read the letter, I just stared happily into space. Aimee was right; we were all truly blessed. And her amazing parents must have shared my thought about writing our story. *They must be so open and loving.* What happened thirteen years ago had been for a reason, and we had the proof in our hands. I was so relieved that she seemed to comprehend at least some of the difficulty I'd gone through trying to decide to relinquish her, even though she hadn't read the letters. I prayed she would read them soon. It was as though she was simply extending her hand to me. I wanted to reach that hand and pull her toward me, but I knew all the moves had to be hers.

I finally opened the letter from her mother, the woman who had made all this joy possible. The woman who was so unselfish that she made room for me not only in her heart and life but also in her child's. So many adoptive moms would understandably be reluctant to reach out to the one woman who could rock their family's world. After all, the adoption horror stories out there were enough to scare any mother. But not this one.

Dear Birthmother,

. . . It's very late and the house is quiet—my husband and I just dug through three to five years' worth of pictures to find just a few for you . . . I've enclosed a letter from Aimee—we finally talked to her about your letters. We felt she is mature enough not to use the knowledge of her birthmother's contact to hurt her sister in some way (sister's birthmother has not communicated at all). At first, when she wrote the enclosed letter to you, she had not read your letters and told us she didn't feel ready to right then. Several days passed, and I mentioned that we would bring copies home (originals were in a safe deposit box) and leave in a designated spot if she ever wanted to read them.

After she read your letters, she cried a little and we talked A LOT. I think she has a good handle on everything, but it was tough to think and really know for the first time that she has half-sisters, plus the reality of your love and concern that she can't reach out and see or touch. Anytime she wants to correspond with you, we'll forward it on. I have never felt threatened by your communication and feel that it's wonderful for Aimee (even if slightly troubling) to know that you care so much.

Her mother went on for six more pages, telling me all about Aimee. Terrific teenager . . . loves little ones . . . cheerleader . . . drama . . . honor roll . . . and then a funny, honest paragraph about teenage angst.

Of course, we have many of the typical teenage thirteen-year-old afflictions— hours on the telephone, violent mood swings, parent bashing, horrible music, etc. BUT, for the most part, we're all hanging in without too much fuss. She is, in short, a very special person, and I'll never have just the right words to say thank you to you . . . Please stay in touch—I know your letters mean a lot to Aimee, and we welcome your love and concern.

Love,

Aimee's Mother

I set the letter aside and looked at Steve. He reached over and took my hands in his own.

"So?" he lifted his eyebrows. "What did she say?"

"She's amazing," I said slowly. "How did I get so lucky to have picked an adoptive mother like her? She is so calm and loving and supportive. She's thoughtful and caring . . . and she's funny." I handed him the letter so he could read it himself and began going through the photos again. I began to think, for the first time, that I might actually meet my birthdaughter and her family someday.

CHAPTER TWENTY-THREE

let's get the party started

I, of course, agonized over my reply. Over the years, Aimee's adoptive mother and I had slowly but steadily communicated. We'd never hurried our responses to one another. Early on, I would write an annual letter to The Cradle, just requesting any information they could give me. That would usually be followed, after a time (sometimes years), by a letter from Aimee's mom. I would then write, rewrite, and perfect a reply, which, with life's interruptions, would always take longer than I planned. I never minded the snail's pace. After all, I didn't want to be a pest. It was a slow but steady process, and that was fine with me.

With each correspondence, I would relish the contents of the envelope: reading, re-reading, and committing each detail to memory. I would respond with great care—thoughtfully thinking through each sentence, each paragraph. This time, however, I was ten times more anxious that my response must be perfect. My answers to Aimee had to be complete, honest, and meaningful. She had to be able to feel my love through my words.

Apparently, she did. Our lives went on, the busy lives of raising three children, working, enjoying precious moments, and all the other parts of daily existence. Two years passed, and then in late 1997, another letter from Aimee arrived, accompanied by one from her adoptive parents. But this time, the letter would change my life, Steve's life . . . it would change everyone's lives.

Dear Mother,

(DEAR MOTHER! Oh my soul, she wrote DEAR MOTHER.)

I never really know how to start a letter to you, but I guess Dear Mom is as good a way as any.

(Yes, darling Aimee, dear Mom is fantastic!)

I thought about typing this . . . but I decided that handwriting is more personal . . . I was wondering, is my handwriting like yours? I was just wondering. My handwriting changes depending on my mood, but I thought maybe it looks like yours.

(Mine changes too! What a funny thing to have in common!)
She went on about getting her driver's license and told me about her new car.

I ended up getting a 1993 Jeep Grand Cherokee. I love it so much. I have been saving since I was ten, so it's strange having no money in the bank anymore. Now we're arguing over curfew.

(Oh my, Taryn is just eleven and has been saving for her car for a year. I can't believe she is writing to me like we've known each other forever.)
She updated me on all her activities and then began the life-changing paragraphs. I kept reading and then skipping back to re-read, as though the words couldn't possibly be right.

How are my half-sisters? I was wondering, do they know about me?

(Not yet, darling. Waiting for the right time.)

I also wonder, what is going on with my birthfather? I have never had any contact with him; I'd like to, though.

(I will tell him, Aimee; I will tell him!)

I would like to have more contact with you, too, if possible. I don't know if you still have AOL or not, but I am an avid emailer. Also, I would like to meet you if that is not something that would disrupt your life too much.

(OH YES, HOW LONG HAVE I BEEN PRAYING FOR THIS? OH YES, OH YES!)

I could barely breathe. This was happening. I was communicating with my darling child, now sixteen years old. She wanted to meet me!

> *I am just so curious about my roots. Not that I am unsatisfied, because I love and enjoy my cousins greatly. I'd just really like to know. And I know I have three half-sisters from you (it was scary how much they resemble me in the Christmas card you sent a few years ago), but what about from my birthfather? You see, I really have no idea!*
>
> *Well, please write back soon. Meeting you would be a dream come true, but I understand that coming back into your life in any major way at this point could be difficult. Just write back, please.*
>
> *Love,*
>
> *Aimee, your daughter*

I burst into tears. How could I process this? Of course I wanted to meet! It's what I had been dreaming about all these years. But to think that she considered it a dream, too—that she was begging me to write back. There really were miracles. And then, a PS:

> *PS: I don't know if I ever said this in the few letters I have written you, but thank you for having me and giving me life and a chance in this world. You are in my prayers, and I thank God for you and the strength he gave you. Anyway, thank you.*

There couldn't be any more tears in my body. Suddenly, I realized it was all worth it. All that agony, all that angst. I would see her again. And she wanted me in her life. And just as importantly, so did her mother. I opened the letter from her and read, wiping my eyes and blowing my nose.

> *Dear Birthmother,*
>
> *. . . Finally, our common interest (Aimee) came into the bedroom last night with a letter she had written to you (enclosed), and I was so glad that she finally got me started!*
>
> *Since your last letter, I've done some reading on adoption and open adoption. Stephanie (from The Cradle) gave me some titles and also The Cradle's position on opening an adoption. Under most circumstances, particularly like ours, they*

recommend it. Apparently, there is no prohibition—if the adopted child and parents agree, then we can disclose the information. Since you gave us your email address, I assume you would be comfortable with exchanging information—if not, you'll have ours, and when and if you are, please give yours!

I laughed at that—she HAD to know by now how comfortable I was with this. She was so similar to me: doing all the research and leaving no stone unturned in the search for the best way to let this all unfold. I flipped over the long yellow sheet of paper and looked at the next page. And just like that, there they were.

So here goes—your birthchild's name is Katherine Anne Stark, "Katie," and we are Temple and Anne Stark. Her little sister is Mary Ellen, and our address and phone number are . . .

My hand was over my mouth. Anne, my beloved grandmother's name. Taylor's and my Mom's middle name. And now my birthdaughter's middle name . . . and her mother's name. Dallas, Texas . . . a phone number . . . how can this be? I guess I was expecting there to be a big process to go through—mountains of correspondence with The Cradle in order to pry open this adoption. But there it was. They didn't live in Chicago like I thought all this time. I don't know why I thought they were there. After all, I knew The Cradle was an international agency. But still, I remembered the feeling of leaving her behind when I went to New York, and all this time, she was down in Dallas!

I've enclosed Katie's letter, which has her email info . . . so I expect you can catch up with all the news on her end via email.

What? Who WAS this woman who was so self-assured and loving that she was comfortable just letting Katie and I continue on our own? I couldn't wait to meet this Anne.

From our perspective, Katie has grown into a beautiful young woman inside and out. She is a joy and delight for us every day. I know she is sad in some ways to think of you and having half-sisters without knowing you. She has a particular affinity for children . . . and she is a loving caretaker.

Anne closed this extraordinary letter in what I would learn to be true Anne fashion.

Hope this isn't too big of a shock. Let us hear from you.
  Anne and Temple

Nope. Not a shock . . . more like a tsunami of shocks. The mother of all shocks.

Aimee was called Katie. Katherine Anne. My heart was full. For so long, she was Aimee, and her parents were "her adoptive parents." Now she had a different name, but still a meaningful name to me. And I finally knew the names of the people to whom I'd handed her to raise. I knew the name of the faceless woman with whom I'd been corresponding for sixteen years. Over time, I had learned about Katie through updates and letters written in stolen hours late at night. The letters got more personal as the years went by, but there was still an anonymous distance, a closed door that kept things careful and detached. Now I knew where she lived. I knew where she went to school. I knew the kind of car she drove, and I knew her handwriting. It was like peeling away layers of an onion only to discover it's the apple you thought you lost.

Andrew and I stayed in touch over the years, a phone call now and then just to catch up. While he was never sure that staying in touch with our child's family was necessarily a good thing, he had been excited when Katie had first written to me a few years before. I called to let him know about all the drama unfolding over the past few days. Like me, he could hardly believe what was happening . . . that our tiny baby was now sixteen years old and reaching out; that we now knew her name and more; that I would be emailing with her, talking with her soon, and possibly meeting her. And then there was big news for Andrew—that she was interested in opening things with him, too. I was thinking only about my excitement, and I guess I probably just assumed he felt the same, but I'm sure it was different for him. This was getting real again, and he had some decisions to make about himself and his family.

Katie's idea of emailing was the perfect way to begin the exciting process of getting to know each other better before speaking on the phone. We began to move forward, testing the waters. Email was kind of a new thing, and we were all just figuring it out, but this was a great reason to become more proficient at it. I sent her a quick email to make sure she had the right address, telling her to write whenever she wanted. As always, I didn't want to intrude on her life, so I waited for her to begin the dance, and I didn't wait long. Her first email arrived, and I was like an excited schoolgirl when I heard that voice say "You've got mail." Katie jumped right in with mundane questions and stories about school—very casual and relaxed. She wanted to know details about our life and then asked some specifics and wrote about her feelings:

> *I was so excited when I got your email . . . excited and confused and all sorts of emotions were going every which way inside me, but it was a happy chaos. I just didn't really know what to feel or think. I guess it's kind of exciting and shocking to get that kind of mail, but I guess you should know, right? I guess I should call you Lorri, right? I don't really know . . . What does your husband think about all this? I know he knows about me and everything, but is he okay with it?*

She went on to ask about our recent trip to Africa and about what to call my parents and then wrote about her recent family ski trip. Then she asked:

> *Please write me back when you get this. I know I sound kind of demanding, but I'm not trying to be. I hope you understand that I am still kind of nervous about this. I guess anxious that you won't write back and that since now I have gotten ahold of you, I don't want to lose you again.*

I smiled wryly to myself. If she only knew how long I'd thought about "if only." If only The Cradle could open the door. If only her adoptive mom would send pictures. If only another update would arrive. If only I could see her. She would know that she could never lose me. It felt amazing to know she felt that instinctive pull, too.

The first few emails back and forth always contained apologies and explanations for any delays. It was Christmas 1997, and we both had many obligations and busy days. I wrote:

> *Dearest Katie,*
>
> *I'm sorry I didn't write back sooner, but to tell you the truth, I checked the email twice a day for the couple of days after I wrote, then decided I shouldn't be so (as you said) anxious, and then with all the Christmas activities going on, I didn't check the mail again until fifteen minutes ago! And guess what reminded me to check? Your birthfather, Andrew, called to ask if I'd heard from you since my email . . . I read the letter to him, and he kept interrupting with questions and comments. My husband was listening, too, and we all felt you sound SO mature.*

Andrew tells me he will send you his picture Christmas card too, and he got his computer from the shop and hopes to figure out how to go online. I told him he's just using that as an excuse (he's slow getting started, and he says he's such a terrible writer that he procrastinates). So, I STRONGLY encouraged him to at least get that card in the mail!

Please don't worry about messing up our lives or interfering or anything like that. You were always such an important part of my life, and Steve is completely supportive. He is an incredible man . . . absolutely the best. Anyway, we will work out this whole process together and make our reunion the best, most positive experience for all involved. Andrew expressed concern over what's best for you. We're all anxious that you come out of this happy and feeling completely loved, because you are, by all of us. We are also concerned to make this totally positive for your parents, who have spent the last sixteen years molding you into the incredible person you so obviously are. And we have to do this in the best way for your half-siblings . . . and that's something we'll have to figure out.

My thoughts are that we get to know each other a little via email—it's such a quick way to communicate, but it gives you a chance to think about what you want to say. It seems that maybe that's a good thing in these initial stages. The next stage should be talking on the phone, I guess . . . wow, that's an exciting thought! And then we'll meet . . . can you believe it? But I do think we should probably do it in these stages, so we are both prepared emotionally. Believe me, knowing me (& I'm sure it's possible that you are as sensitive and emotional as I am), it will be an emotional time. But also one of the most important and satisfying times of my life.

With all my love,

Lorri

It was a happy, fulfilling time. Checking email was an elevating experience every time I'd look and see her email name. She would fill my mailbox with daily activities and news. She told me Andrew sent her an overnight package with a gift and pictures of her half-siblings.

It is so neat that I have five little brothers and sisters and that I have cousins. Do your sisters have any kids? I don't have any first cousins over here. My dad is an only child and my mom has an older brother who never had kids.

She told me all about her friends—their names, their relationships, and how exciting all of this was for them.

I have always been so proud of being adopted.

(Kudos, Anne . . . what a marvelous statement that was!)

That is usually what I say when I'm in a new place and you have to go around the circle and tell something about yourself. So my friends all knew and now they are all really excited for me. Anyway, we have decided that you look a lot like my friend Hailey's mother . . . you are so beautiful. All of this makes me so happy, I don't know what to say.

Then . . . some questions . . .

Where did you grow up? Where did you go to college? When you had me, did you get to hold me before you made your decision? I know, I have so many questions, but I guess these are just thoughts that have been unanswered for so many years. I am so glad that we are doing this . . . I told you my friends' names just because much of my life revolves around them right now, and I want you to feel like you are a part of my life. I love you!

I sat at the computer quietly and then said a quiet prayer of thanksgiving. *Thank you, God, for letting this happen.*

The correspondence continued—exchanging information, asking and answering questions. Sometimes time would pass—my girls would have a rush of activities, Katie would have tests or school plays or cheerleading—but then an email would appear with an explanation and more inquisitive interrogations or detailed stories. Katie told me about her first fender bender, and I told her the story of her birth. We consoled one another when we both lost a beloved elderly relative within weeks of each other. We discussed coincidences and the impending first phone call. I wrote:

My dear Katie,

I'm ready when you are. I know you technically reached out to me first, but I made a firm and absolute promise to your parents that I would never interfere in your life or search you out . . . that I would leave that to you. That if it was what you wanted and your parents wanted, then I was 100 percent interested

in bringing our lives together. Because of that promise, I think on principle
that you should initiate the call, this first call anyway. I would call you this
minute, but I think it has to be your move . . . for everyone's peace of mind. If
you write and ask me to make the call, I will, but again, I would like you to call
the shots . . . I'm really excited to talk to your parents, too—I feel like I know
your mother after corresponding with her all these years!

Waiting with lots of love,

Lorri

Later, Katie told me about being in the bookstore and reading a poem from
the book *A 3rd Serving of Chicken Soup for the Soul.* She said she started crying
right there in the bookstore. She sent it to me, and I knew she was my daughter.
I was crying before I was halfway through.

THE LEGACY OF AN ADOPTED CHILD

Anonymous

Once there were two women who never knew each other.
One you do not remember, the other you call Mother.
Two different lives shaped to make you one.
One became your guiding star. The other became your sun.
The first one gave you life; the second taught you to live it.
The first one gave you a need for love; the second was there to give it.
One gave you nationality; the other gave you a name.
One gave you a talent; the other gave you aim.
One gave you emotions; the other calmed your fears.
One saw your first sweet smile; the other dried your tears.
One sought for you a home that she could not provide,
The other prayed for a child and her hope was not denied.
And now you ask me through your tears
The age-old question, unanswered through the years.
Heredity or environment. Which are you a product of?
Neither, my darling. Neither. Just two different kinds of love.

just a phone call away

ndrew was slow to get online, which delayed his communication, but Katie didn't seem to mind. She was just happy that the connection was there. I would relay a message to one or the other from time to time, but eventually, they started their own email train. She and I told each other good times to call and reassured each other of our interest, but the call didn't take place for six weeks. Katie was worried about calling at the wrong time and either accidentally reaching one of the girls or not having time to do it right. I began to worry and secretly wonder if she would really call. Years later, Katie admitted that she had called many times and then hung up, too anxious to actually talk.

I had expressly told her it was her call to make. I had waited sixteen years for this phone call, however, so finally, unable to hold it in any longer, I expressed a bit of my angst over the delay in an easy, casual letter. It was mid-February, 1998.

> *Dear Katie,*
>
> *So much time is going by between our correspondences, I'm starting to get a tiny bit nervous. I'm afraid that this tremendous event which has occurred between us is going to get lost in everyday life and obligations, and that would*

make me sadder than I can express. I know I'm bad, too, in letting so much time go by and letting our crazy schedule interfere with staying in touch with you, and I'm going to try to do better . . . I know that you have school obligations and that you are a busy teenager with a million things to do, and these pauses are probably nothing more than that. It's definitely the case on my part.

Anyway, as far as I'm concerned, I am ready to have our first talk on the phone whenever you are. I've given this lots of thought over the last few months, and we can develop our relationship first before I need to involve your sisters, and that's really been my only concern. I think I will speak to a child psychologist or counselor to get some thoughts on the best way to let them know they have a sister. I think I told you that I had always thought I would tell them in their early teens, but now I don't think we can or should wait that long. I just want to make sure this is a wonderful, positive experience for everyone . . .

I love you,

Lorri

A night or two later, after the girls were in bed, Steve walked into the office we shared with the phone in his hand and a knowing look on his face. My eyes grew big and my jaw dropped as he handed me the phone.

"Hello?" I said tentatively, listening intently to hear the sound of my teenage daughter's voice for the first time since I'd heard her newborn cry.

"Lorri?"

It was perfect and joyous and amazing, and the next day, she sent an email about how incredible it was to talk to me, her birthmother. I answered her immediately:

Dearest Katie,

You're right; it was wonderful to finally have the long-awaited phone call. This all certainly ranks right up there with the best moments of my life. I'd thought about it for sixteen years, and to have it happen is even better than I could have imagined. You sound so great . . . so happy and full of life, opinions, and energy. And talking to your mom was so great, too. The conversation really confirmed what I've felt all along . . . that she is an unusually giving, loving, and empathetic person.

It's funny; since we started emailing and getting to know each other and after all the letters back and forth from your mom, I've felt this to be an incredibly positive, loving, and uplifting experience for all of us. Very unusual.

And I've thought, maybe this was all meant to be, to bring these two families together somehow. It seems that there are so many similarities and just such positive energy that maybe there's a connection—deeper, more than just the obvious. Anyway, those are my somewhat mystical or spiritual thoughts of the moment . . .

   All my love,

   Lorri

In another email a month later, I addressed some of the complicated sentiments that all of us were experiencing, including Andrew.

Dear Katie,

   Andrew called me today . . . we had a great talk. He said he got your email message to him mentioning that we had talked, and he was full of questions about how that went. You should get a call from him soon . . . he said he was very excited to talk to you. He really is interested in talking and meeting with you. He was anxious to hear all about what we talked about and how you sounded, what you were like. This is just a very exciting time for all of us.

   It's funny . . . we are all so positive and feeling good about all that has happened, and yet time goes by between our communications. There's a part of me that wants to hop on a plane tomorrow and come see you and another part that holds me back, makes me think things through, wants to do this one step at a time, very carefully. I'm not sure why. It's what I've wanted since you came into the world, and yet I just want to make sure everything goes just right. I think Andrew feels some of these same things, and you too, actually.

   All I know is it will be wonderful when the time comes.

   I love you,

   Lorri

By April, we had had our second phone call, and it went as well as the first. Katie was vibrant, so easy to talk to, and full of energy. We had talked into the night about the possibility of a book on our story. And we talked about telling her sisters the news that somewhere out there was another sister. As I'd mentioned to Katie, I had always thought I would tell the girls my story as a cautionary "it can happen to you" lesson when they reached puberty or the age of getting interested in the opposite sex. Now that a reunion was in the near future, that plan was off the table. NOW would just have to be the right time to hear the news. I researched the topic with my new and less-than-impressive Internet skills, and in June, Steve and I decided to tell eleven-year-old Taryn first.

Dear Katie,

Well, we did it! Steve and I sat down with Taryn and told her the whole story. She took it well and is so interested in all the details, especially about you now. We tried to take her through the story, filling in the blanks and letting her know about all the emotional aspects along the way. I took out my folder with all the correspondence and photos from over the years, and we went over lots of it. We had some teary moments, but, as I suspected, she is really excited and thinks it's great. She is such a special girl, a lot like you, and she seemed to grasp the whole saga.

Doesn't seem to be any real trauma in her acceptance of everything. She is just thrilled to know . . . she thanked us for telling her and is upbeat and happy. Isn't that great? We're planning to tell the other girls on our trip up to Ohio this weekend. We thought we'd have a long ride to talk about everything together. After telling Taryn, I'm starting to think Halli may be the toughest one, because I really don't know what she'll understand. Well, we'll deal with it!

I love you,

Lorri

I was wrong. Neither five-year-old Halli nor nine-year-old Taylor had one problem with the whole concept. They were both ecstatic. Their reaction was wonder and joy and laughter. They couldn't wait to see Katie and talk to her.

Hey, sweetie!

Well, guess what! We told the other two girls about you in the car on the way up here from Naples. It was great—everyone is just excited and thrilled and looking forward to meeting you! All the things I was worried about, the possible scenarios, they're not happening. They can't wait! One funny story . . . I was telling the girls, and, every now and then, I'd start to cry, you know, the emotion of everything. About the third time I started crying, Taylor, in her compassionate way, said, "Mom, if you're going to keep crying, maybe we should just change the subject." We were just hysterical—we all burst out laughing . . .

Now everyone knew the big secret. There was just one thing left to do.

d-day

1998

Our reunion was planned, fittingly, on my birthday weekend, October 2–4, 1998. This was the best present I could ever receive. Not that it came about easily. Just like the phone call, we went back and forth discussing when it might happen, wondering how the other felt, making suggestions, and running into roadblocks. Would I go to her, or would she come to me? I sent Katie one email expressing my fear that because of our crazy schedule, I may have not seemed as excited as I was.

Dearest Katie,

I feel like I have not expressed myself well at all with this whole getting-to-gether thing, so I want to tell you clearly . . . meeting you is something I've dreamed about for sixteen years, and I can't wait!!! It must seem otherwise, since there seems to always be some timing problem, and it's just not true. Being the perfectionist that I am, I want the timing and the whole thing to be just right. I want you to know you are welcome here anytime, the sooner the better, and we will accommodate your schedule as best we can. We can keep planning my visit, and that's fine. It's just more complicated with making sure the girls are covered, Steve's schedule, etc., but it will happen. Even so, if you ever decide you want to come here, that would be fabulous, and we even have a guest room

that's always ready for you. If you feel more comfortable coming with Anne or
Temple or your whole family, that's great, too. Whatever works for you.

I guess I feel like I'm looking for this perfect time when we're both completely
free, and that will take some planning. And I wanted you to have this open invi-
tation . . . anytime, my home is your home, and that goes for your family, too.

Sending lots of love,

Lorri

Katie answered that she was definitely thinking of coming to Florida, rather
than doing the reunion in Dallas, as that would give her the opportunity to meet
her sisters and Steve as well. We finally zeroed in on my birthday weekend. She
kept me apprised of the progress, picked the date, and ordered the tickets, and
then, during the third week of September, she alerted me that the tickets had
arrived. This was happening!

The anticipation was incredible. Steve was almost as excited as me, and the
girls were bouncing off the walls. I'd now spoken to Katie and Anne several
times planning the trip, and the conversation was getting easier and more comfortable and familiar with each phone call. The strangeness and nervousness
were both a thing of the past, and now it was just a matter of counting the days.
Suddenly, it was Friday of the reunion weekend, and Katie and Anne were on
their way! Of course, not without drama! They called from Miami, and the five
of us jumped up when the phone rang. They were almost here! But the news
was that bad weather had caused a missed connection in Miami, and there
were no more flights to Naples that night. They would figure out their next
move and call back.

I looked at my family and gave them the news, and my supreme disappointment was mirrored in each of their faces. *Really?* Sixteen years wasn't long
enough—we would have to wait another day? I sank down in my chair. A flash-
back to November 1981 appeared in my head . . . tiny Aimee on my bent legs as I
sat in my hospital bed . . . looking into her lovely eyes as she gripped my pinkies
with her miniature fingers . . . my last anguished look at her as she disappeared
with the nurse. I felt the sharp pang again, reminding me of the agony I felt then
and the hope I'd been living with ever since. I was on the brink of seeing those
eyes, those fingers, that face. I just couldn't wait. And then the phone rang again
with a new plan. They would not be here at eight twenty tonight as planned, but
the determined Starks had rented a car, would grab a bite to eat, and then would

start the two-hour drive across Alligator Alley. They thought they would arrive around midnight.

We gathered the girls up to bed, promising them that the fun would be full speed ahead in the morning. And then Steve and I sat and waited, the pent-up anxiety showing in both our faces. I hadn't gotten much sleep the two nights beforehand, and now I had the makings of a cold. But I was way too hopped up on my own emotions to relax, let alone nap. Getting up every couple of minutes to peer out the window at our driveway, I thought about how many times I had imagined this day. It was inconceivable that the moment was almost at hand. Would it be awkward? Would we know what to say? How would I ever take my eyes off her?

Suddenly, at midnight on the dot, lights flashed as a car came up the driveway. Steve, always thinking, grabbed the video camera. I grabbed nothing, thought nothing, and could barely move. I was paralyzed with the sensations of the moment. This was it! We walked to the door, and Steve opened it just as Katie and Anne hurried up the walk.

"Hold on there," Steve joked, "let me get the video tape rolling!"

Katie and I stared at each other, taking in every detail of each other's features, and then big grins shot across both our faces. She picked up speed and threw herself into my open arms. The last time I'd held this child was sixteen years ago in my hospital room. In the blink of an eye, she was grown. There was no way I would be holding back tears that night! We hugged and rocked, laughed and cried. Oh, dear God, every one of my prayers was answered in that instant. And after an eternity, I looked over Katie's shoulder and saw Anne, standing there watching through tears, with a warm, satisfied smile on her face. Her child was fiercely hanging onto the only other person in the world she could conceivably call mother, and there stood Anne, so happy for the two of us. I took Katie's face between my hands, kissed her on the cheek, and introduced her to the man behind the camera. Then I turned to Anne and threw my arms around her. I owed this woman everything.

Suffice it to say, the weekend was sensational. The only downside was I did end up sick with laryngitis, so I wrote the following email to my parents and sisters who were waiting impatiently for every detail of the reunion.

Dear Mom, Dad, Linda, and Kim,

Well, since I have absolutely no voice whatsoever, I thought I'd send you

all an email about Katie's visit . . . It was a whirlwind weekend, and we tried
to cram so much into a few hours. She is an absolute love. That was great that
it was my birthday, and you all called and got a chance to say hello to her. You
can see how effortless it is to talk with her. She smiles all the time and is full
of life and personality. She really looks a lot like Andrew, but there's definitely
Antosz in her too.

Anne, her mom, is an utter dream. It's clear to see where Katie gets the
easy-to-talk-to trait. Anne makes conversation flow like you've always been
friends. And maybe part of that is it seems like we always HAVE been friends.
We talked about that a lot: how we felt like we'd always known each other.

It was such a shame about their flight Friday night; they didn't get here
until midnight, but they were in great spirits, and we sat around and Anne
and I had a glass of wine (you'd love her, Mom; she shares your passion for a
pre-dinner "taste of the grape" as she says), and the four of us talked until two
o'clock in the morning. I showed them to their hotel, and we called it a night.

Uncertain about how things would go, Anne had felt it prudent to stay in
a hotel, at least for this first visit. And while it made perfect sense, we all hated
to have to pack them up and send them off at two in the morning. I led the way
so they could find the hotel easily, and then we called it a night. Early Saturday
morning, I had a quick, impossible-to-cancel obligation with Taylor.

It worked out okay because Katie, being sixteen, relished the idea of sleep-
ing in, at least a little, and Anne wanted to go for a run on the beach. We
agreed to have them come back to the house around ten thirty the next morn-
ing. Anyway, they arrived with a huge armful of flowers for my birthday—
just beautiful. You all called right in that time period that we were hanging
around the house, so that was fun for her, and we looked at my baby pictures
of Katie and some of my papers and letters and stuff about her and then at
some of the pictures Anne and Katie brought of Katie as a baby and growing
up. They were wonderful. You can just see the happiness. Anne was explain-
ing who the people were, where the pics were taken, etc., and it became clear
that their family is a lot like ours: very close, animated, family oriented, and
lots of fun.

They were very interested in going to the beach, so we packed up and went
to the beach, got our spot situated, and went to lunch at the Ritz Grill right
there . . . It was a perfect beach day; we rented a little paddle-kayak and

just relaxed, talked, took pictures, and had fun. We didn't want to leave but finally went back to the house, had a glass of wine, looked at more pictures, and then realized we had to hurry or miss the sunset, so they left to shower and change.

We missed the sunset by a few minutes, so we decided to go down to Olde Naples to the pier to catch the afterglow. Then we went to Tommy Bahama's and had a great dinner. I opened presents from Steve and the girls . . . and gave Anne a mother/child sculpture to thank her for taking such good care of this precious child. Then I gave Katie a pretty heart locket necklace to remind her that she always has been in my heart and she always will be. It was very emotional but very wonderful.

After dinner, we went back to the house and had birthday cake, got the girls to bed, finished the last of the pictures, and went in the Jacuzzi for a little while. We stayed up until one thirty in the morning, and then they went back to their hotel. This morning, we picked them up for nine o'clock Mass. It was a very nice Mass and had particular significance because this marked the beginning of Respect Life Week.

It was a reminder to all of us that Katie was here and this whole miracle had come about simply because of the decision I'd made those many years ago.

After Mass, we went to the Skillets Café for a super brunch, and Steve's parents came and joined us.

The farewell at the airport was quite teary. We took video and more pictures, and then Katie started crying, and soon, we all were weepy. As they got on the plane, Halli stood against the window and cried. It was very touching. Taylor and Taryn really wanted her to stay longer. They all seemed to bond so easily. We feel really lucky . . . what a tremendous blessing.

First reunion, October 4, 1998: the sisters, Taylor, Taryn, Katie, and Halli

First reunion, October 4, 1998: Lorri, Katie, Taylor, Halli, Steve, Taryn, and Anne

We hope we'll get together again soon, and I'd love to include her in the family reunion we are talking about having. I wrote an email right away, and I'm including it below. Gives you a good idea of how we felt throughout the weekend. I love you all and will of course keep you posted.

Love, Lorri

I had sent Katie an email when we came home from the little Naples airport, just trying to express what the weekend had meant to me.

My dearest Katie,

What an emotional time at the airport! Seems like everything we'd been feeling over the weekend came bursting out. The girls are crazy about you, and little Halli stood by the window sobbing when you got on the plane.

This was such a whirlwind of a weekend . . . I hope it wasn't too overwhelming for you. We really can't expect to catch up on almost seventeen years, actually our whole lives, in one weekend. There are still so many things to talk about, questions to ask, topics we didn't even get close to exploring. I hope we have many other opportunities to spend time together.

You are everything I could have hoped a daughter could turn out to be. You are so bright, loving, and beautiful, and to see you with the girls was a dream come true. They all love you already; it was pretty amazing how easily you all fell into place together.

This weekend helped so much to reassure me about my long-ago decision. Your parents have done such an incredible job raising you to be thoughtful, compassionate, caring, and inquisitive, and I could just go on and on. Of course I will always think about how it might have been, but I wanted the best life for you, and from what I can see, it doesn't get much better than what you have. I absolutely adore Anne, and I feel as though we were meant to get together and develop our own relationship. She is truly someone special, and I look forward to meeting Temple and Mary Ellen, too. I know they will also be special people.

When you think about all the people out there, how blessedly lucky [for us all] that Anne and Temple were the ones to get you. They seem so much like my own family: so open, affectionate, and close. In fact, as you all were describing your family get-togethers and vacations, I kept thinking, That's how my family is and how Steve and I are making our family. It may be asking a lot, but I hope in the years ahead, our families can all get to know one another and be close. It feels so natural to me. Like it was meant to be. Almost like you were the conduit to bringing together a group of people who should naturally be friends and family. It's pretty amazing.

> *I will write a letter to your mom, since I know she doesn't go in for email, but let her know how much I loved this weekend. It was much too short, but maybe just enough to give us all lots to think about and look forward to . . . Thank you again for the gorgeous flowers. They will remind me all week of our fabulous weekend. . . . As I told you Saturday night, you have always been in my heart, and you always will be. I hope the heart necklace will remind you of that, because it's important that you remember how much you are loved. Our reunion is really that—a way of bringing together the people who love you.*
>
> *Well, that's it for now, but I will write and call and stay in touch. I have to get some rest—you wore me out, girl! But what a great weekend.*
>
> *I love you, Katie Anne.*
>
> *Love, Lorri*

Katie wrote back right away, expressing a lot of the same sentiments. She talked about the excitement of her friends when she brought pictures and stories from the weekend. She talked about how they thought we looked like each other and even how Anne resembled me in some ways. And she said she missed us.

> *Dear Family,*
>
> *I miss you all so much. It is kind of hard that now that I know you and my sisters, we have to be so far apart. I can't wait to get together again and to meet your parents and sisters . . . Anyway, tell Taryn, Taylor, and Halli that I am thinking about them all the time and that I love them.*

It had been an experience that had transformed us all. So much so that when it was time for Katie to begin applying to colleges, she wrote her college essay about her personal reunion experience:

> I could barely keep my eyes open. We had been traveling for nearly twelve hours, thanks to weather delays. As we drove through the unfamiliar neighborhood, I sat up straight and my stomach began to roll. I turned to my mother and squeezed her hand. Our journey was almost over, but our lives were about to change forever.
>
> Squinting in the dark-we are both pretty night-blind-we found the house. I ran a shaky hand through my hair, tried to make myself look presentable, and stepped out of the car.

Before I even made it up the walk, the door was open and she was waiting with open arms. I took one look at her and I knew. Finally, after nearly seventeen years, I was looking into the eyes of the woman who had given birth to me.

This reunion of birthmother and adopted child had been years in the works. My mother and my birthmother, Lorri, had corresponded anonymously for fifteen years. I chose to begin the process of opening up the adoption, and the letters finally became personal; I learned her name, where she lived, and all about her family. The next step was talking on the telephone. I was terrified as I lifted the receiver to dial the first time. As close as I felt to her through the letters, I didn't know what to expect one on one, over the phone. My fingers shook as I dialed those ten unfamiliar digits, and my heart began to pound. The phone rang once, twice . . . three times, a voice answered, and hesitantly, I said,

"Hello . . . um, is Lorri there?"

"This is Lorri."

"Oh, um . . . this is Katie-your daughter."

"Katie! I can't believe it's you! I am so glad to hear your voice."

Relief rushed over me, and again I was at ease and as comfortable as I had always been with my unusual situation.

A few months and many telephone calls later, I decided to make the trip to Florida to meet Lorri. Great anxiety and confusion coursed through my body as we stood in the doorway and looked at one another. Then she hugged me, and, at once, I knew that I was so very lucky. Not only do I have one amazing mother: I have two. One who loves and trusts me enough to travel with me to meet the woman who many would see as a threat to our relationship. And another mother, in a different sense, whose love was so great that she gave me up to people who could give me the life she couldn't provide at the time.

So I stood there between these two remarkable, selfless women, who have so much more in common than just me, and realized how much I can learn from them. One has shaped me by heredity, the other by environment, and both by my extraordinary experience of their great love and sacrifice.

In all my perfectionism, I could not have planned the weekend to be more perfect than it was. When we talk about it now, there is one funny moment that stands out. It happened on that late Friday night after the emotions had run their course and we were settling into conversation. Steve and Katie were standing over at the kitchen counter talking when Katie glanced over at Anne and me on the couch, wine glasses in hand, in the family room. We were deep in conversation, talking as though we were long-lost best friends. We were intent on each other's comments, touching each other's hands, and throwing our heads back in laughter. It reflected a friendship that was familiar and easy, one that had begun sixteen years earlier.

Katie turned to Steve and, with a wry grin, remarked dryly, "And I thought this was about me."

one family

O ur reunion was the birth of a new extended family. We stayed solidly in touch through the phone and email. Our next visit was planned a few months later, so we could meet Katie's sister, Mary Ellen, and adoptive father, Temple. The family was going on a vacation and would be flying through Miami with a hefty layover. This would normally be a pain in the neck, but it created an excellent opportunity for another reunion. We drove across the Alley with much anticipation and a little case of the nerves. Katie's sister, also adopted, was opposed to the idea of meeting her own birth-family and told Katie she thought she was crazy to open up this can of worms. And Temple, content with his life and adopted family, had never sought out his own birthparents. We weren't sure that we would receive the same kind of welcome as we had from Katie and Anne, but we were all excited to just put the real people together with the names and pictures we'd seen.

Any worries we had were gone within moments of gathering in the Admiral's Club meeting room that Steve had reserved. Mary Ellen was a darling fourteen-year-old girl, and before she knew what hit her, my girls and their innocent exuberance had made her one of the sisters. And Temple was one of the warmest, kindest, and funniest men I'd ever met. He might not have made the same decision for himself, but when Katie made the choice to bring us into their lives, he fully supported her in every way. He was a jewel of a man, and I liked him instantly.

The following summer, in 1999, my parents hosted a family reunion for their children and grandchildren in Estes Park, Colorado. Our family decided to turn the trip into a month-long car trek around the country, visiting Steve's family in Ohio and stopping to see family and friends as we made our way west. Katie flew out for the occasion, and we couldn't wait to pick her up at the Denver airport. It was nothing short of amazing, the way she just dropped in the middle of all the cousins, aunts, uncles, and grandparents as though she'd known them her whole life. After a week of hiking, softball, archery, white-water rafting, and a million other activities, not to mention just hanging out, eating, and talking, Katie was firmly ensconced in the Antosz family. It was a magical time with many tears and much laughter. She then joined us on our return drive, stopping at my former boss's house, the executive producer of *Donahue*. After being a part of the initial drama, Pat McMillen was thrilled to meet Katie and hear all about the happy ending. From there, we drove to Santa Fe and then all the way to her family's cottage on a lake outside Dallas. We joked that if we could make it through a road trip across West Texas together, we could make it through anything.

Lorri and Anne, Possum Kingdom, TX, August 1999

Taylor, Taryn, Katie, Lorri, and Halli, Possum Kingdom, TX, August 1999

Katie and Lorri, Possum Kingdom, TX, August 1999

Halli, Lorri, Taylor, Anne, and Taryn, Possum Kingdom, TX, August 1999

Our relationship with one another grew closer without much commotion, awkwardness, or drama. We did many an airport rendezvous, including a surprise Christmas visit in Dallas. We were flying through Dallas on our way to Phoenix on Christmas Day 1999, and I arranged with Anne for us to pop in and surprise Katie for a couple of hours. On that visit, we met Katie's grandparents—the much-talked-about Imie, Granny Barbara, and Granddaddy Travis. Each time we saw each other, we felt more and more at home.

This began the habit of staying at each other's homes, remembering birthdays, going on trips together, and calling just to catch up and tell each other big news. It was the most natural, flowing process: a seamless transition from strangers to family. No one panicked or worried about how things "should" be anymore—it just was.

Taylor, Anne, and Temple, Dallas, TX, December 1999

This is not to say there were no hiccups, no small missteps that took place along the way to becoming one family. It took me several breakfasts with strawberries before I knew not to serve Katie the berries that would make her break out in hives. She was equally allergic to our beloved housecat, who always managed to sneak in and hide under her bed in the guest room. To her credit, she was good-natured about the inevitable congestion and sneezing, but I always felt bad that her allergy symptoms were a part of every visit to our home. And I couldn't seem to remember that Katie didn't have pierced ears—it took me two or three gifts of earrings before I caught on that her ears still weren't pierced.

For the most part, however, things started easily between us and just got easier.

Steve, Halli, Taylor, Katie, Mary Ellen, Lorri, and Taryn, Captiva, FL, March 2001

Taylor, Katie, Halli, and Taryn, Naples, FL, May 2001

Katie's desire *to know* extended to her birthfather. I facilitated her first meeting with Andrew, which took place in the Dallas airport: another airport rendezvous. While their relationship didn't catch fire as fast as ours did, they did carve out a fond friendship that worked for both of them. When Katie graduated from the University of Texas a few years later, Andrew flew to Austin to be there and support her with the rest of us. It was the first time I'd seen him in seventeen years, the first time for Steve to meet him, and certainly the first time for Katie to have her parents and both birthparents together in the same place. That night, we all dined under the stars and twinkling lights, celebrating Katie's graduation. But I was secretly having my own little celebration, too, thinking how wonderful it was that we could all be together after everything we'd been through, and after so many years.

Steve and I also grew closer and closer with Anne and Temple. Our family would meet up with their family, and while the sisters disappeared to do what sisters do, we would just hang out together—learning about each other and discovering how much we really liked one another. Temple shared Anne's talent of turning a story into a tale that left us gasping for breath and hopeless with laughter. He also shared her generosity of spirit, and his big heart welcomed us without question. We knew him just long enough to dearly love him before he was diagnosed with early-onset Alzheimer's disease at the age of fifty-four.

Katie was with our family on a short vacation in the Keys when Temple received his diagnosis. That was one of the few trips together when things didn't seem quite right. I couldn't put my finger on it, but there was an uncomfortable tension at times that made me wonder if we'd done something to make her unhappy. As it turned out, Anne and Temple wanted to wait until Katie was home to tell her the

Taryn, Katie, Taylor, Halli, Steve, and Lorri, Florida Keys, August 2000

shocking news in person, and while she couldn't identify the bad feeling, she just knew she needed and wanted to be home.

Our family was very present as Anne, Katie, Mary Ellen, and Temple went through the discovery and devastating reality of Temple's affliction. I will always thank God that we had the privilege of knowing that magnificent man, and we tried our best to be part of the support team when the illness began to inflict its damage. When he passed away a mere seven years after his diagnosis, we faced that tragedy as a family. While Temple would never be replaced, I was always happy that Steve was in Katie's life to provide a shoulder, fatherly advice, or whatever she needed from him. Katie lived for a time in Los Angeles, and when Steve would come out for his monthly meetings, they would always meet, just the two of them, to share a dinner and solve the world's problems.

The times together that cemented what we had into a *forever family* were varied. We grieved together at Temple's funeral, and we danced at Mary Ellen's wedding. When Taryn decided to marry in a very hasty, very small ceremony on the beach, I called Katie to tell her and also to reassure her that it wasn't necessary to fly in. She had one question.

"Is she wearing a white dress?" she asked pointedly.

"Yes," I replied, "but . . ."

"But nothing," she interrupted. "I'll be there."

After that first Colorado Antosz family reunion, we began a tradition of summers in Steamboat Springs that continued for sixteen years. I don't think Katie missed but maybe one or two of those special times. I had to give her a lot of credit. She dropped in to an entire family and had to find her place. People looked like her and acted like her but essentially were strangers in the beginning. She described it as an "otherness"; she was a member of the family but still separate. She had to figure out her role, how she fit in, and how the rest of us saw her, all at a relatively young age. Our journey toward blending and

connecting our families was certainly simpler for Anne and me. This was something I wanted from the moment Katie was born, and Anne had a curiosity and open heart that welcomed more love for her daughter. Katie was a teenager, and very brave, and that courage kept her striving to want more.

Katie and the Bensons in Colorado, July 2002

When I became G-Lo to Taryn's two little boys, Katie also got a new name . . . Aunt Katie. She relished her role as aunt just as she reveled in her role as big sister, giving out sage, sisterly advice to her younger half-siblings.

The one thing I hadn't done was meet one of Katie's boyfriends. I talked to Anne about it, and she was just as perplexed.

Lorri, Katie, Halli, Steve, Anne, Taylor, and Mary Ellen, Possom Kingdom, TX, August 2002

"She has lots of friends who are boys," she explained, "but not many who are boyfriends, and even when I know she is dating someone, she doesn't bring him home." And then Katie met Alex in business school, and just like that, everything changed. Anne told me she thought this was the one. The two of them found themselves on the east coast of Florida one weekend, so Steve, Halli, and I drove over to meet the now-famous Alex. I'm not sure how he felt having to meet the approval of not one mother but two, but just the fact that he took the whole unusual situation matter-of-factly made him a winner in my book. Turns out Anne's prediction was correct—Alex was the one for our Katie.

full circle

It was June 2, 2012, an amazing day of anticipation for every single one of us. Katie and Alex were getting married! They had decided that their union would take place in two parts. They wanted part one to be an intimate, immediate family–only affair. This would be a Catholic Mass service in a small chapel, followed by a lovely dinner atop one of Dallas's finest hotels. Part two would take place two weeks later in Austin, Texas where many of their business school and college friends were located. It would be a large, more casual party/reception.

When Katie first called to tell me her plans, I immediately assumed we would be making arrangements to fly to Austin. Then she went into the details of the plans.

"If the girls can't get off work or can't afford to fly in for both events, I will understand. But if I have to choose, I really want them at the first one, the wedding and dinner. That will be the real wedding, and I want my whole family there."

I was silent for a split second. She wanted us? All of us? At the immediate family–only event? I was touched beyond expression. I loved Katie and Anne and the rest of the Stark clan with all my heart. They were family to me. But to hear that she wanted us there, to complete her immediate family . . . well, there were no words . . . but somehow, I found some.

"Oh, Katie," I said quietly, choked with emotion. "We will all be there, of course. Steve and I will be at both events, and we'll see if the girls can do both Dallas and Austin, but they will definitely be in Dallas on June 2!" As always,

I wondered about the generosity of spirit displayed by Anne, who of course knew about and endorsed Katie and Alex's plan. The only people at the wedding event would be parents, siblings, and grandparents. No cousins, no aunts or uncles, and no friends. And Anne supported Katie's wishes to have her birthmother's family present.

There were times throughout that day when I would just stop and take a mental snapshot of what was going on. The moms and daughters all gathered in a large hotel suite for hair and makeup, Halli and Taylor got the tunes playing, and the dancing started. It was like music for my heart to watch the five sisters, relaxed, laughing, and enjoying the female rituals together. Their rapport was so natural . . . just like any other family. Thirty years earlier, I'd just hoped I'd know who Katie grew up to be. Never in a million years did I ever dream it could be like this.

The sisters, Taylor, Katie, Halli, and Taryn, June 2, 2012   *Lorri, Katie, and Anne, June 2, 2012*

It was a very intimate ceremony. The chapel was tiny but cozy, and each of us was given a part in the ceremony. Steve and I did readings, and Alex's mom and Anne did the Prayer of the Faithful. Taryn, her husband, and her baby Leo brought the gifts to the altar, and Taylor, Halli, Katie's brother-in-law, and Alex's sister-in-law provided the music. Taryn's oldest son tried his best to steal the show as ring bearer, and we stopped the action one time for Anne's mother to powder her nose. The ceremony was warm, spontaneous, and familiar . . . and just right.

We had looked forward to this special wedding, but I didn't realize how powerful the day would be until after Katie and Alex were married and we were all sitting around the long reception table in the

Lorri and Katie, June 2, 2012

beautiful private dining room that night. One by one, we each got up and gave a heartfelt toast to the bride and groom. At first, I didn't want to be so presumptuous as to stand up and speak, but it soon became clear that everyone would take their turn. After all, there weren't that many of us. I stood, glass in hand.

"I am just amazed as I look around this table at this wonderful group of people," I began. "I realize that of the sixteen people present, over a third are Bensons!" Steve and I, our three daughters, and our son-in-law were gathered with Katie, Alex, Anne, Mary Ellen and her husband, Daniel, Granny Barbara, and Alex's parents, brother, and sister-in-law.

"I can't tell you," I continued, "how blessed and honored I feel to be here tonight, as one family. The days when I was pregnant with you, Katie, and the time afterward were the darkest days of my life. It's not been easy over the years, living without Katie, but the pain pales in comparison to the happiness I feel tonight. Having you, Katie, as part of our family the last few years has been a dream come true, and this is the cherry on top. Steve and I and our family are thrilled to share in this beautiful celebration of love."

I went on to tearfully toast my birthdaughter, my darling girl now grown into a stunning bride. And her husband, so in love, and perfectly suited to his new wife. I continued my emotional toast with words for my adored husband and my girls, whose support, love, and acceptance of Katie had made bringing our lives together as seamless as the sky. And then I looked at Anne.

"And I'd like to finish by raising a glass to Anne," I said solemnly. "To a woman who has been the most amazing mother to Katie and a true, unexpected dear friend to me. She and Temple were everything I ever wanted in parents for Katie, and Anne has always been such an example of love and selflessness—a perfect role model for Katie. Her generosity, confidence, and giant heart made room for us in their lives, and it's why we are all so

Lorri's toast to Anne, June 2, 2012

close and why we are even here tonight." I lifted my goblet in her direction. "To our fantastic host, dear Anne. You are one in a million."

There wasn't a dry eye in the room. Because this was such a unique group, there were lots of tears after most of the toasts. After I spoke, I sat and listened to

Lorri's reflections during wedding toasts, June 2, 2012

the other tributes, looking at the faces around the room. It was profound. An unbelievable, peaceful joy washed over me . . . a feeling of completion, of wholeness. We WERE immediate family. Thirty-one years after Katie's birth, we were, once again, immediate family.

As the dinner drew to a close, I walked over to Anne and gave her a giant hug. She hugged me back, and then, in typical Anne fashion, she said with her fabulous Texas drawl, "How 'bout our daughter? Isn't she beautiful?"

She sure was. And so was her mother.

epilogue

O n March 3, 2015, our adoption story added another amazing chapter. Annabel Elizabeth Knight was born, Katie and Alex's firstborn child. When I first laid eyes on this glorious child at four weeks, I couldn't help but think back to the sorrowful day when I signed the adoption papers. But now, that sad memory makes perfect sense. The story has come full circle with the birth of this magical little girl, and now,

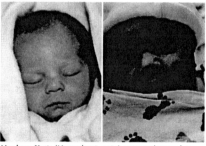

Newborn Katie (November 8, 1981) compared to newborn Annabel (March 3, 2015)

like before, Anne's generosity knows no bounds as she shares her grand-child with G-Lo. As she has always been known to say, "The more love, the better."

I have wanted to write this book for a long, long time. I mentioned this to Anne in a very early letter back in 1995. Ever since then, it has been clear that somehow, through a miraculous act of God, Katie was meant to stay in my life and our families were meant to become one. I know there are tough stories out there. I know there are people on all sides of adoption relationships who for their own personal reasons do not want or need a totally integrated birth/adoptive family. And I know people have been hurt during reunions and attempts at communication. I am not such a Pollyanna that I don't know ours is an unusually positive relationship, but I hope it can inspire more adoption stories to have happy endings. I believe that if each party involved has the right approach, the right outlook, and a giving and generous heart, there can be more of these close and loving outcomes.

Perhaps the primary reason for the success of our adoption story is Anne's attitude and tremendous ability to love and to be secure in that love, but many factors worked in our favor. Steve has been remarkable, from his first immediate acceptance of the situation to his easy and loving reception of the Stark family into our lives. He and Katie have been close from the beginning, and the two of them have their own relationship apart from me. To find someone so tolerant and accommodating was divine intervention.

My girls and Katie's family have all made this a comfortable transition from separate families to one family. They accepted each other and the situation without question. They never for a minute seemed unsure about how any of this would affect their place in their family but instead focused on how these new relationships would enhance their lives. As children, the five newly-minted sisters did not fight anything but rather simply bonded as though it was the most natural thing in the world.

And Katie has been spectacular from the moment her curiosity began moving her toward a reunion with me. Her maturity, delightful smile, courage, and welcoming personality made everything as smooth as silk. As Anne said in one of her letters, "Katie is a trusting soul, and fortunately, none of us let her down." She welcomed each step with enthusiasm, inquisitiveness, love, and wisdom far beyond her chronological age.

But none of it could have developed without Anne's rare outlook. From the beginning with the first letters, I have felt a special and unexplainable bond with Anne. When we finally met, that feeling quickly grew. It felt like a meeting of our souls. That first weekend together with Katie and Anne brought such a feeling of peace. It finally all made sense. It seemed clear that I went through the trauma of giving Katie up for adoption so that she could be with Anne and Temple and so she would, someday, bring us all together. It seemed like Anne and I were meant to be in each other's lives, and Katie was the link.

Certainly, there are situations where birthparents and/or adoptive parents need to maintain their privacy or keep their identities secret and the adoption closed. But from my experience, I would venture to say those cases are rare. Today, the majority of adoptions are open; perhaps not to the degree that ours is, but more open than ours started out to be. I would offer that many COULD be as open as ours, and the key person is the adoptive mother or father.

I don't hide the fact that I have a birthdaughter; I speak on the subject. More often than not, adoptive parents will come up afterward and tell me that they would be too afraid to allow their child's birthparents to play such a role in their lives. Based on my experience with Anne, I would have to guess that they may not feel secure enough in their relationship with their child. I know that's a harsh statement to make. But in my experience, the key to the success of our relationship was that Anne never doubted who Katie's mother was. She never worried that Katie would use the knowledge against her, even when Katie, in a teenage rage, once said, "You're not even my real mother." Anne was smart enough to know that Katie was just trying to say the one thing that would hurt her the most. She recognized in her gut that Katie knew who her real mother was.

As a birthmother, I knew my decision was final and that I was rolling the dice hoping that Katie's new mom might give me a small window into their lives. Throughout the process of reconnect- ing and developing our place in each other's lives, I made every effort to respect Anne's boundaries and place as Katie's true mother. I believe this is another important piece of the puzzle. I had no idea what the odds were for that to happen. I never expected to win the jackpot and actually end up as one fam- ily. But we did. And for that, I have to thank Anne.

Lorri, Anne, and Annabel on the Santa Monica Beach, 2016

acknowledgments

Thank you to my Familius family, including Christopher Robbins, who recognized this book's value and had the vision to turn one book into so much more. Also to my clever editor Michele Robbins, who made editing not only bearable but a breeze. I lost both my parents within a month of each other during the book's editing, and I can't say enough about the kindness, love, and patient support shown to me by Christopher, Michele, and the entire staff at Familius. Thank you also to Chris Eyre of Legacy Ventures, who takes paying it forward to a new level. To his brother Richard Eyre, thank you for lending a hand to a fellow writer and taking the time to make a connection. I am eternally grateful to Phil Donahue for his beautiful words at the beginning of this book and for the privilege of having him in my life now and as my boss years ago. Thank you to The Cradle, who from day one to present day has been supportive, compassionate, and professional; even in the toughest days, I felt that they cared for me and my needs as much as those of my daughter and her family. To Steve Benson, my rock and my soul mate, I will never be able to express what your support and love means to me. Thank you to my three daughters, Halli, Taylor, and Taryn, for our amazing relationship and your loving help during this project. A special shout out to Taryn, who took time during an exceptionally busy period in her life to examine the manuscript and give copious and insightful notes and commentary. Thank you in memory of Leo and June Antosz, who were there for me my whole life, no matter what, showing me what was important. And "thank you" does not cover the gratitude I feel toward Anne Stark and Kate Stark Knight. They are the heart of this story, and they are my family. Their love and generosity, and that of the whole Stark/Knight/Benson clan, gave our story the "happily ever after" ending we enjoy today.

about the author

Lorri Antosz Benson is an award-winning television producer, writer, author, and former internationally syndicated columnist. She worked for *Donahue*, the acclaimed show hosted by the legendary Phil Donahue, for fifteen years, eight of which were spent as Senior Producer. Lorri received two Emmy Awards and ten Emmy nominations for her work with *Donahue* and was awarded the American Women in Radio and Television Commendation.

Lorri and her daughter Taryn coauthored the book *Distorted*, a memoir delving into her daughter's struggle with an eating disorder. They were featured on several national broadcasts, including the *Today Show* and the *Montel Williams Show*. Her work has led her to become a family advocate and a speaker/expert on eating disorders and resources for parents. She serves on the Parent, Family & Friends Network steering committee for the National Eating Disorder Association and contributes to their webcasts and newsletters.

Lorri and her husband Steve reside in Santa Monica, CA. They have four children and three grandchildren.

P lease stay tuned for the second book in our three-part series on adoption, coming out in 2017. *Fifty Ways to Love Your Child—A Manual for Birthparents, Adoptive Parents, and Adoptees* will be an informative and exciting book of advice and suggestions for all those involved in adoption. The experiences of Anne Stark and Kate Stark Knight will be added to those of Lorri Antosz Benson in this collection of secrets, lessons learned, and firsthand anecdotes of what works and what doesn't in adoptive relationships. Their personal recommendations will be augmented by contributions from other birthparents, adoptive parents, and adopted children, including celebrities and top stars. Learn about topics such as:

- How and when to tell your child they are adopted
- What an adopted child needs to hear from their adoptive parents
- How to have the optimal mindset BEFORE you adopt
- How a first/birthmother can build a life after placing her child for adoption

For the first time, all three perspectives of a highly effective open adoption story will come together to help provide a primer for adoption success.

about familius

Welcome to a place where parents are celebrated, not compared. Where heart is at the center of our families, and family at the center of our homes. Where boo-boos are still kissed, cake beaters are still licked, and mistakes are still okay. Welcome to a place where books—and family—are beautiful. Familius: a book publisher dedicated to helping families be happy.

Visit Our Website: www.familius.com

Our website is a different kind of place. Get inspired, read articles, discover books, watch videos, connect with our family experts, download books and apps and audiobooks, and along the way, discover how values and happy family life go together.

Join Our Family

There are lots of ways to connect with us! Subscribe to our newsletters at www.familius.com to receive uplifting daily inspiration, essays from our Pater Familius, a free ebook every month, and the first word on special discounts and Familius news.

Become an Expert

Familius authors and other established writers interested in helping families be happy are invited to join our family and contribute online content. If you have something important to say on the family, join our expert community by applying at:

www.familius.com/apply-to-become-a-familius-expert

Get Bulk Discounts

If you feel a few friends and family might benefit from what you've read, let us know and we'll be happy to provide you with quantity discounts. Simply email us at orders@familius.com.

Website: www.familius.com

Facebook: www.facebook.com/paterfamilius

Twitter: @familiustalk, @paterfamilius1

Pinterest: www.pinterest.com/familius

The most important work you

ever do will be within the walls

of your own home.

CPSIA information can be obtained
at www.ICGtesting.com
Printed in the USA
FSOW01n2305200716
22943FS